Praise for *Doing More with Teams*

"Piasecki does a superb job at outlining the origins of the team-work paradigm and its relevance to our lives today. He recognizes its application to business and offers great advice for creating a teamwork inspired atmosphere. *Doing More with Teams* is an insightful book and a must-have for anyone wanting to create an effective and dynamic workplace environment."

—Erol User
CEO and Founder of Istanbul's User Corporation

"Rarely has a person accomplished so much, navigated such waters, and reached so high, and still remained accessible and generous enough to share the wealth of knowledge he gained along the steep journey. He has unlocked in this book a wealth of secret truths and translated them into a shareable language we all need to learn. A Renaissance Man, Piasecki has bridged the prodigious communication gaps between the business world, the people, and the realm of social needs."

—Hadassah Broscova
Editor-in-Chief, *Carpe Articulum Literary Review*

"Read Bruce Piasecki's book, *Doing More with Teams* not because it's an interesting read, but because Bruce has decades of experience actually getting teams to do more. I have seen Bruce use his passion, sincerity and creative world view to harness a bunch of Type A executives from different backgrounds and get them going in a new and exciting direction. Learn from someone who loves ideas, who loves people and who loves to bring the two together to accomplish great things."

"More often than not, we tend to lose sight of the simplest truths, in both our business and personal lives. In the sequel to his bestselling *Doing More with Less*, Bruce Piasecki helps us to retrain our sights on these basic truths, enabling all of us who depend on teams to lead by example and ultimately succeed."

"Hot on the heels of *Doing More with Less*, Bruce has produced *Doing More with Teams* where he skillfully lays out the value of working together to achieve greater outcomes. Paired, they are a valuable resource for creating a resilient future for individuals and organizations."

DOING MORE WITH TEAMS

DOING MORE WITH TEAMS

THE NEW WAY TO WINNING

BRUCE PIASECKI

WILEY

ISBN: 978-1-118-48495-1 (cloth)
ISBN: 978-1-118-63160-7 (ebk)
ISBN: 978-1-118-63167-6 (ebk)
ISBN: 978-1-118-63168-3 (ebk)

Printed in the United States of America

10 9 8 7 6 5 4 3 2 1

Contents

Acknowledgments

'll offer an icy page of thanks, since today is exceptionally snowy.

From the icy Adirondack high country, where alpine itself is defined in splendid flora and frigid fauna, near my homestead and AHC Group offices, to the Navy SEAL teams that abound in mud, mosquito rich swamp, and sweltering heat, teams surround and surprise us.

This makes writing inclusive acknowledgements to what inspired this ninth book of mine rather impossible.

My family forms the most formidable team I have been blessed to encounter.

You will see thanks to my now deceased mother, my wife Andrea Carol Masters, and my daughter, as well as my extended family, in these forthcoming pages—and for good reason. My earliest sense of fairness in teams and the excitement of competition for attention and result derive directly from these early family experiences.

Family gave me the confidence and space to explore now five decades of teamwork—this includes insights from four years of competitive League One Varsity high school basketball, track (where the shot put holes stayed in my Mom's backyard for years), to where the ceaseless running as my team's center halfback in soccer kept me in shape to start the basketball season all over again.

And this love and attention to team and teamwork kept me at it during the 30 years of making, growing, and mastering my firm—the www.ahcgroup.com. In fact, I now see how the first allowed the second—how competitive sports formed the values in competitive consulting. For the last 30 years as a management consultant, I have met each week with new and amazingly complex teams in full splendor or in serious need of realignment.

Since 1981, I have been, in effect, the captain of my firm as we function daily as a team. You will see each of my Senior Associates and key staff in Appendix A.

I thank again my literary agent William Gladstone, the founder and force behind Waterside Productions, and I thank my speaking agent Shawn Hanks, the chief operating officer and force behind Premier Speakers.

The ultimate visual dictionary of thanks to teams, in my life, would prove vast. For all my past teammates, at last this book.

DOING
MORE
WITH
TEAMS

Winning without Weapons

A Preamble

There is something about teams that expands our experience of being human. Teams extend our wings, in practical, pragmatic, and measureable ways.

And when done right, this experience of teams makes all of us—those in Asia, Africa, Europe, or North America, rich or poor—feel more humane, more competitive, and more contributory to a shared near-future than ever before in our personal or family lives. Why is this?

In the military, we call this achievement from teams "shared actionable understanding" or the shared trust, vision, and coherence of all members of a team. In this book we explore many different kinds of teams, from corporate teams to Navy SEALs to the Boston Celtics. And in each case, we derive the essential oils that bring a smooth set of actions and results to teams.

Why is this smoothness important?

And why does this extension of what is human really matter to us?

Why, for example, does soccer become the most important and popular world game?

We suggest it has to do with the certain magical facelessness of an entire team effort evident in each soccer game, no matter what the level of play or what nation it is played in. In contrast, "solo" performing teams—that is, teams like those based on an autocratic "first face" such as Lance Armstrong's recently denuded Tour de France cyclist teams—age faster in our appreciation and memory.

Why is this? It will take this full book to answer by explaining this miracle of social history.

Let's take this issue of team facelessness from the opposite point of view. Why do the select few in basketball, the supercharged superheroes of the National Basketball Association (NBA)—folks as iconic as Kobe Bryant and King LeBron James—lose some of their appeal and their approachability as they become larger than life? We loved them in college or high school, but afterward, we view some with distance and dislike. These men mean less to many of us than our own teammates over time. They might become as famous globally as a Charlie Chaplin, but the love they are granted is shorter lived as others replace them when they retire.

So what is the special sauce that keeps team fame as individuals wane?

As their special 1 in 10 million skills become even more exceptional, more superhuman, some basketball stars have fallen beyond our daily sense of achievable joys and hopes. These basketball demigods shrink like aged photos before our eyes in time. In this way, they become like so many of our number one best sellers in music and pop art—kings for a day, not a decade.

Of course, there are loved exceptions such as the Boston Celtics and the San Antonio Spurs, which are loved for a long time by millions.

This book will examine more closely these more commonplace players for the special ingredients we will call team coherence and team integrity.

Why is this pattern discernible in so many corporate and sports settings as well? There are many firms where the chief executive officer (CEO), who appeared to be respected by all, is hated upon after only a few months of departure from the first. In contrast, team-based CEOs can seem built to last; they keep our respect over decades. Could it be, for example, how they handle their tales of the team?

And why might business leaders good at using the metaphors of teams excel well beyond the norm?

Beyond Determinism

You will not find the answer if you think only like those such as Sigmund Freud or Karl Marx. Freud and Marx were clearly two of the three greatest thinkers at the apex of industrialism in the nineteenth century, the third being Charles Darwin. But they all overlooked something very important.

For more than 100 years now, these two gifted thinkers helped create a feeling of determinism to individual lives and helped shape our overall understanding about industrial competition and personal growth. They created the folktales of industrialism that still feed so many of our popular assumptions about work and play.

And yet both Marx and Freud were profoundly uninterested in the establishment, appeal, and satisfaction found in teams.

Freud believed all human lives boil down to ego; the animal instincts he called the id; and civilization's call, which he termed the superego. The id, ego, and superego were, to Freud, the three fuels that fed human motivation, human understanding, and human ambition. Freud wrote more than 20 beautifully argued books indicating why he believed these engines within the self predetermined our successes and our failures, our families, and our friendships.

Yet he was profoundly inept when it came to team formation, the wisdom in teams, and how to achieve results in a swift and severe world of circumstance and hardship.

It would be more generous to say, as many intellectual historians before me, that in the age of Freud, Marx, and Darwin—and nearly a hundred years after them—the importance of teams was not fully recognized and was more often ignored as they searched for their secret sauce in human motivation and fears.

There is a profound need for acceptance in the human drama, and teams provide the most accessible platform for its exploration and maturation.

Although elites like Freud, Marx, and Darwin from the past century often outlined elaborate paths of self-discovery, reversal, and triumph in a modern lifetime, my point here is grander in its simplicity: teams abound and always will. They are as much a part of human aspiration as seeking three meals a day.

The missing links in Freud are now more obvious. Those in Marx and Darwin are a bit more hidden and more difficult to unearth. Marx, for example, in his brilliant essays, such as "Wage, Labor and Capital," was equally wrong when it came to teams. He argues that owners are not interested in anything deep down but the means of production.

Marx essentially argued that only if you have the means of production could you enjoy success. And every day, teams prove this narrow and uninteresting.

Marx believed that owners exploited the labor power of individuals in order to control more of the means of production. It never crossed Marx's mind, or pen, that many on teams would pursue raising the performance of all players, raising, as we note in business, "the boats of all in the marketplace" so as to benefit our standing and our selves. This rising of aspiration and expectation in team play abounds everywhere, from sports to firms to the military—as the tales in this book show. It is very different than the imperatives of a labor union or the general assumptions Marx embedded in the proletariat. In teams, we extend beyond class, economics, and many related forms of determinism. How you play matters much more than where you come from in teams!

What is hilariously clear now about these predominant nineteenth-century views of social determinism is how ignorant Marx and Freud became—as all of their contorted brethren since—regarding the common magic of teams.

This book, then, is designed to remind us of what many organizations that thrive share—from churches and mosques to sports clubs to corporate units to special forces to large military organizations: namely, the power, the logic, and the smart inclusiveness of teams.

A Dynamic Example

My uncles Mike and Steve first told me about the 1939 Ukraine soccer team called Dynamo over a Thanksgiving dinner outside in our shared backyard.

Steve was married to my lovely Ukrainian Aunt Anna, and Mike was the great family storyteller, a bare-knuckled boxer when he first came to Newark from Poland, and one known to exaggerate for effect.

So I listened to this tall tale of a great football team's astonishing results against the invading Nazi with both fascination and polite suspicion.

It turned out to be true, forming in my early mind a great example of the simple nobility in teams and how society invests so much in them over time.

Hitler had already invaded our homeland in 1939. And by June 1941, he was still able to astonish and confound with a fierce focus not understood by the average European in power.

In fact, in the few short months of this tale, Hitler made his greatest military gains in all of World War II, conquering Ukraine, his largest single country to take in a few bloodstained months.

When the capital city goes, the people's pride and spirit often begins to dissolve. A people's collective identity frays and severely fractures when their capital falls. Conquerors since Alexander know this instinctively.

By June 1941, Kiev was circled, assaulted, and completely overrun. Family members describe it as a shell of its former self, hollowed in a way reflected by the great works of the time. Key members of the city's defenders were captured, tortured, or incarcerated—including each of the members of the famous 1939 Dynamo Kiev football team, which some argue was the best squad of well-equipped men in Europe before the war.

The team was shattered, hungry, and scattered.

Three Features in Exceptional Teams

There was a quiet Ukrainian bakery owner who made all the difference in the world. He recognized the once-charismatic goalkeeper of the Dynamo squad, as he wandered, head down, disheveled, and in disarray one day along the lonely streets of his motherland's capital.

The baker offered Trusevich, the goalkeeper, a job and some shelter. And soon enough, other teammates were invited in. As they made bread for the Nazis, they were fed bread both as workers in the bakery and as guys who let off steam at the end of the day by playing what they loved to play—European football, Soccer with a capital S.

After Kiev had been occupied for a few months, a Nazi strongman had a brilliantly stupid idea: Why not set up some matches between the locals and the occupiers as a way to entertain and get everyone's minds off the tension and the pain?

A series of very public matches were arranged, and each time the tired underdogs, because of their skill and something deeper, won—humiliating the Nazi team. There was a terrifying vividness to each score, as something larger than pride of ownership at stake, evident to both those in the stands and those on the restless streets of Ukraine.

Andy Dougan retold this story in his recent book *Dynamo*. He reminds us how football has the power to galvanize nations. As alert citizens, we saw this again in the summer of 2012 as the world witnessed the Poland versus Russia world football game. We recall it in the very famous set of games that helped Nelson Mandela bring South Africa back to life. The pattern goes back to ancient Olympics in Greece and the near East.

Dougan notes, in extended passages, how games express political will and social yearning through large tangible amounts of symbol and competitive longing.

But what Dougan does not underline, sufficiently in my mind at least, is the recurrent, commonplace, and extraordinary power we find in teams. He focuses on the games and the drama of the games, not the meaning of teams. He makes these players special, when, in fact, they became famous and mattered to so many because what they did was in all of us.

And that is what matters about teams.

About Eminent Men

What matters about teams is how commonplace the feelings about them are. Underdogs can win. The downtrodden can rise. And at times, even the most brutal opponents can lose.

Let's explore this cluster of feelings in humans as constituting a magic in teams. I use the word *magic* quite deliberately, in a fashion used by anthropologists and when courts of many nations find themselves investigating motives deeper than ordinary socioeconomics.

This need for us to believe in a near-future both more just and more available is what sustains us, and it is what I mean by making us more human and what I mean about how teamwork extends our wings.

For those of you who know the story, the ending cannot remain in triumph.

Even when the games were being refereed by SS officers, the Dynamo spirit won again and again; by the end of 1941, they had become a living allegory of both resistance and the ordinary.

And here is my point deeper than ordinary psychology and more extraordinary than ordinary Darwinian animal behaviors. Bravery is a complex thing, and the voice and velocity of triumph can be stopped short, as evidenced by the Nazis who came to the bakery and slaughtered like pigs select team players. We also saw this coming all along, but never did we need to stop short—the team had its destiny, and it was a new kind of winning.

What my family remembers is the rightness in their victory, and many uncles and Eastern European aunts spoke with personal pride about each of the players. I write this now so that future members of my extended family can find ways to remember this tale of the Dynamo as well. In teams we mature, and in teams, we grow.

Today, I know enough to call this winning without weapons.

I dedicate this book to those who know how important this remains in a world of 7 billion souls.

Winning without Weapons: Summary

★ Teamwork expands our wings and allows for "shared actionable understanding."

★ Karl Marx and Sigmund Freud's idea of individual determinism lacks of profound satisfaction achieved when part of a team.

★ The Kiev 1941 Dynamo soccer team is an example of how teamwork has the power to galvanize nations.

★ Even "underdog" teams have the ability to win through commonplace and extraordinary shared power.

What Makes This Century Severe?

1

To Be Young Forever Is No Fun

There is a false correctness in how the world celebrates youth and how modern life celebrates individualism.

What makes this world so severe to so many is this over-reliance on youth and individualism. As I now am in my late fifties, I can say this with some force and fascination to those concerned about making teams that last.

To be young forever is no fun. This truth begets a gentler stronger truth. Those who survive across four to nine decades are often those who have fun in teams. Those who outlive the follies of youth engender a nexus of principles that enables the celebration of good teamwork, and these near-future trainers prepare the new kids on the block for this classic understanding of good competition.

What is miraculous to me is how much of this team building happens outside the classic nuclear family.

Why Youth Itself Is Not the Answer

Let us step back first before we continue forward with these book-length claims.

Youth and individualism are leading concepts that form our sense of identity and our faith in competition. They are the modern cornerstones of most of us.

They form the very foundation stones of modern consumerism.

You can see these forms of celebratory youth and individualism from Madison Avenue flip-flops worn by urban male

50-year-olds to those bold yellow-lime swimsuits meant for younger bodies that abound on the Long Island beaches I roam.

The same fashions found on the beaches in Sydney, Australia; Singapore; and Japan can be found on the beaches of Long Island, Brazil, and Los Angeles.

The fashion industry is simply the most extreme case of something we all notice when watching TV, while riding in planes and on trains, or when talking with the suburban educated elites that populate most high-tech firms. The rapid devaluation of Facebook as its billionaire founder brought them into public valuation is another example of this overvaluation of youth. The stock value decline that occurred for months after the initial public offering (IPO) cost the owners of the stock tons. But this devaluation was inevitable, because this bubble of youth cannot last. The firm was not maturely run yet as a coherent team; it was too top-heavy.

Popular industrial culture celebrates youth and the chance for individuals to buy into a consumptive individualism. But the false correctness in all this fancy cannot last long.

Youth Irritates; Teams Mature

If we scratch one skin level deeper than this surface consumerism, we see something else beneath.

Everyone I interviewed for this book can recall the details of how young athletic males got to keep secret sins during their youth while continuing to enjoy sustained family and pubic praise—all because they were triumphant contenders.

We will call this *The Macho Paradox* (deliberating taking and extending the term in the book by the same title).

The public is often outraged by these behaviors of favoritism and special advantage, and historically, there has been a strong backlash against these pimpled celebrities when they burn their teams as well as their colleagues. But why is this?

This arrogant license, this self-assured margin of error, assumed by youth outrages many. I think it is because this forms the opposite of team play, and the great masses want to see the bubble of the improbable pop as a grand cultural act of rebalancing.

Resentment against these youths who rapidly rise to the top often feeds further outrage when these same youths hit the market-place after college. Most newspaper sports sections, for example, are half full of tales of super-competitive individuals caught in scandal. I see this social process—which we can call the MVP paradox—not as sport but as public anthropology. In contrast, over the past several centuries, we have celebrated the hard-fought rags-to-riches stories of folks such as Franklin and Kevin Garnett, perhaps because their success did not happen in a snap.

Our reading of history is really quite simple: the sublime elements of human aspiration often fall into traps rendered anew in this swift and severe world, unless this aspiring individual stands with others, for a few seasons, and matures through the magic of teams.

The Disadvantages of Individual Greatness

The MVP paradox is about the presumed status of past achieve-ments. Here a former most valuable player has trouble adjusting to a new situation, both because of all the baggage he or she carries into the new team and because of unique disadvantages found in individual greatness.

Most of us believe that a way to outlive these bundled problems of youth is through teamwork. Teams somehow mature even the reluctant.

These social value systems in teams seem to help round off that special edge of youth in practice for many of us, into a higher social value. It sharpens our skills and responsibilities. I see this as a clear result of teamwork in my life and firm.

Often during a key staff hire interview, where five or six of us have two finalists in mind, I will relax the interview testing and ask the finalists, "What was your best team experience?" Those whose answers include real context that illustrates the team dynamics, not just their own individual feelings, have often turned out the best hires in our firm.

In the end, we come to understand that to be young forever is no fun compared with winning as a team. My point is as eternal as the stages of humans: youth irritates; teamwork matures.

The Hourglass of Our Short Lives

We learn through teams how to suspend our individual time clocks and flip over the hourglass of our short lives into a state of play where each grain of passing sand adds up to a sense of purpose larger than ourselves.

Notice the change of tone as we move away from the individualistic terms such as *Macho Paradox*, *scandal*, and *hidden errors* to those of teamwork such as coherence, integrity, and captains. Once this shift is made, the world becomes more intelligible, more acceptable, and less stressed.

After writing this section of the book, I took an afternoon off to return to my favorite books. When I flipped through the many biographies of famous men and women, skimming many decades of marginal comments or underlined points of emphasis, I noticed how many of the subjects on my shelves became famous because they had a great supporting team of family and friends.

This is really the main point of most biographies.

Mere mortals become larger players through teams. The sheer nature of most humans thrives on this kind of recognition. How did we allow Sigmund Freud, Karl Marx, and Charles Darwin to miss all this for so long?

Near Futurte Training Tip

 We learn through teams how to suspend our individual time clocks, and flip over the hour glass of our short lives into a state of play where each grain of passing sand adds up to a sense of purpose larger than ourselves.

For more leadership insights, visit www.ahcgroup.com

Another Sense of Time: Social Time

In my management practice, I often work with executives responsible for teams exceeding 1,000. I study why and how they work. Often, the leader says that giving a common direction is the ultimate glue creating team unity.

In this way, teams defy ordinary time. They give us something bigger than individual motivation.

And in the assignments of team tasks and in the rituals of group accountability, we see a kind of energy in teams that gives us a glimpse of eternity, a way to stop ordinary individualistic attitudes and behaviors so that we can transform work time into playtime.

Here are a few introductory examples of how superb teamwork changes our perception of time.

The Power in Teams

One way in which teams are magical is that they allow all different types of people to succeed. People who would not normally be able to succeed on an individual basis can reap the benefits of success and reach peaks they would not be able to climb alone.

For example, the natural-born leader will thrive in a team setting, because he or she has the ability to project the work of their teams contributions to the team out into the public arena, filling the stands and the stadium. The beauty of teams is that even though the born leader may be able to succeed individually as a result of his or her own innate instincts, that same leader feels better and more fulfilled when the success is shared.

The Useful and the Honorable

The rest of the team—the planners and the doers, the specialty players and the substitutes—are often people whose creativity and contributions may go unnoticed because they do not have the internal spark to market themselves or stand out like the natural-born leader.

Nonetheless, the mix of differences meld, and as the group comes together, the team becomes one as it triumphs.

Here is the magic that teams bring to all ranges and types of people. Whether you are studying the 1920 Yankees, the 1950 Canadians, the 1960 Packers, or the 1990 Chicago Bulls, the magic of teams transcends youth and individualism.

The best teams are diverse in age, experience, and abilities. They have an abundance of team integrity and team coherence, which we discuss further in later chapters.

In addition to discussing a team's ability to synthesize differences, this book explores how teams allow even gifted individuals to feel better about themselves. Perhaps one of the reasons literary history is full of tormented storylines of Edgar Allen Poe, John Keats, and even my modern superhero George Orwell is that so many creative greats have worked in relative isolation, for a patron, or for a distant editor, without the daily pleasures of working as part of a team.

Teamwork allows the gifted and the less than gifted to learn together where they fit. In this book we will explore this fitness in teams, this smoothness we have all felt at times, and look forward to understanding it a bit more.

It was pure pleasure for a decade, for example, to watch how Michael Jordan fit within his court family. Like a true Shakespearean family, his team included not only the multi-faceted talents of Scottie Pippen, whose grace and quieter excellence could withstand the daily scrutiny and praise to Jordan himself. It was a deep family, and a family full of different personalities. Dennis Rodman, who was such a rebounder and such an immense impulse player that his performances allowed thousands to look past his outrageous off-court behaviors. Even today, more than a decade after their amazing feats of competitiveness, I remember those Jordan, Pippen, and Rodman games where the trio made a 10-person team absolutely stunning. I remember, with some hesitation, that Rodman dated Madonna, and I think he had some amazing tattoos. But I more clearly remember his team play and his feats of balance on the court.

The stand-out eccentric genius of Rodman as a great rebounder is often missed when you have Jordan and Pippen playing in tandem, but upon serious examination, you see that the Chicago Bulls went 10 players deep, each with a distinct set of talents and skills known and exploited by a coach who was both a past player and a mentor.

Legacy teams require this depth and this bridging of extreme individualistic differences.

Here is the main point: the great teams allow you to see your strengths and work consistently on your weaknesses, and they allow you to share in the shoulder strength of others moving forward.

In management consulting, this ability to facilitate the shared shoulder strength, what the military calls shared actionable understanding, is the very essence of corporate alignment and change.

Tips for Near-Future Training: An Aside on Sharing Shoulder Strength

Near Future Training Tips

 All great teams share shoulder strength; they have diversity, depth and range in their talent, not just one or two superstars.

 Military teams that work best achieve this "shared actionable understanding" with remarkable regularity through extensive training and team building.

 You can do the same by starting with the arts of competitive frugality, and make your team do more with less.

For more leadership insights, visit www.ahcgroup.com

The great teams, such as the Dynamo (see the Preamble) and the Jordan, Pippen, and Rodman Chicago Bulls, shared shoulder strength. They have diversity, depth, and range in their talent, not just one or two superstars. The military teams that work best achieve this shared actionable understanding with remarkable regularity through extensive training and team building.

You can do the same. It's best to start with the art of competitive frugality. This will help you battle for balance. But over time, what settles the score for you is finding the right team and swimming in the right ponds that bring you a sense of place. For more on this struggle to achieve freedom and your fate in teams, see www.doingmorewithlessbook.com.

Beyond the Arrogance of Youth

In this book we explore how the life cycle of teams is far more lasting and far more interesting than that of any individual—no matter how heroic or strange. Sociology becomes the only fully accurate biography in this sense.

In teams, we live from game to game, from season to season, and do not, if we measure the success of teams, age as only individuals.

The next chapter makes this point by looking at the stages of an individual life, trying to squeeze out the secret sauce in leading teams. And in the final chapters of this book, we look at the life cycle of teams by applying the first third's principles to teams in action.

Why, for example, did those Jordan, Pippen, and Rodman Chicago Bulls dominate the 1990s, like the Yankees dominated the 1920s? The patterns are recurrent. And what is there today in the Boston Celtics that creates such fascination and chemistry in such a set of different players?

Toward the end of this book, we need to ask the question of all questions: Why is there this fascination with teams if youth and individualism are the preferred characteristics of our popular culture?

At this point, let me fast-forward to a possible answer: this fascination with teams is based on the opposite of existential dread, the dread that we will die.

Instead of the dread and severity found in rampant individualism, the magic and power of teams is based, deep down, in a functional awareness in ordinary time that good teams are common, recurrent, and the very essence of being human. This is nothing super-heavy or unconscious. When we are feeling good watching teams, I think it a celebration of this recurrent human feeling, this sense of a continuum in teams.

Some Self-Reflection

Why has this issue of doing more with teams become so precious to me? Perhaps it is because I have now celebrated the thirtieth anniversary of my marriage, of my firm, and of my books?

No, after some reflection, I do not think the occurrence of this anniversary is sufficient to explain the full depth of the feeling I think we all share in teams.

I think now it is because aging makes sense when seen in the context of society and teams. The passage of time is inevitable, and we first understand how fleeting it is when we do our best in a 48-minute basketball game, for example. But we do not need to feel this anguish as annihilating. In teams we sprout wings and our fight reaches beyond our first expectations.

The next few chapters explore how this notion of extended wings can be understood, both as we age and as we come to know what team play means.

I have learned that there is more lasting satisfaction in being part of teams and peer groups more from the teams themselves than from my own aging process. To be young forever proves no fun compared with being part of the triumph of teams. To be radically alone proves quite dreadful in the end.

This is a set of higher facts in the human experience we all share. But why is this so visible in teamwork?

Animal Magnetism

I live near a town known for its horses, history, and health. Saratoga Springs has many horse stables, plenty of informed horse people, and many tall tales about high rollers and horseplay.

One thing I've learned from this town is that you cannot buy a winner or train a winning horse without having an elaborate support team. Some think they can do it alone, and they often go broke.

People in town tell me that a horse responds to a quiet consistent confidence in its handlers over time, and there is a belief that the more valuable a horse is, the less they respond to immediate demands. Like great athletes or strong soldiers, great horses are built by teams, coaches, and owners over time, not in a season. They know the signals before a race that matters, and they know how to relax after a race.

So when I think about the training and development of great horses, my mind sometimes wanders to the development of high-performing executives. Are they not similar to thoroughbred stallions?

Great business executives often see themselves as the makers of teams. Now, don't get me wrong. Some chief executive officers (CEOs) I've worked for and some whom I have studied are exceptional egoists, and they see the world as if they made the team—with the emphasis on the "I not only made this team, but I run this team." But most of the ones who last many races and persist over that fierce test of time are more like thoroughbred stallions. They know how to run among many well-trained competitors. These executives know to take the turns in a measured way, how to sprint when necessary, and how to run hard to the end.

But there is an important characteristic of modern superior executives that is very different from that of the prize-winning colts. They are matured through seasons by team play, and they are very rehearsed in giving credit to the team. The self-aware high performer is also, in my experience, an exceptional team player.

J. Richard Hackman of Harvard on Teams

Without a doubt, the theorists of teams are mounting a robust attack, offering a spectrum of frameworks to appreciate what we all can see. From leadership scholars such as John Kotter to Warren Bennis, everyone is in the game of studying exceptional teams.

One of the best at creating a big-picture framework to see teams form is Harvard professor J. Richard Hackman. His book *Leading Teams: Setting the Stage for Great Performances* is a well-written and well-received scholarly account of the preconditions that allow successful team play.

I like to think we all have dipped our fingers into the real-life glue these five phrases suggest of team success:

1. **The team must be real.** It cannot exist in name only. You cannot dictate teamwork from above or through ownership. *Real* means the team is competitive.

2. **The team must have a compelling direction for it to work.** This is bigger and more immediate than ordinary corporate visioning of purpose. It is compelling to the point of team members not noticing exhaustion and working well beyond ordinary measures of speed, strength, hand-eye coordination, and so on.

3. **The team must have an enabling structure that facilitates teamwork.** I find in corporate consulting that this is a real differentiator. Good governance of owners, coaches, and players allows this, whether you are a senior Navy SEAL or a chief financial officer reviewing cash flow. In Chapter 4, we present a case study on Shaw to underline this feature.

4. **The team must operate in a supportive organizational context where fans and players and owners and coaches mix well.** The smoothness we explore is not one-dimensional. In other words, the team on the field is only one cell in a complex semipermeable membrane of organizations.

5. **The team must have an expert in teamwork coaching.** This is the major missing link in most groups aspiring to be creative teams.

I call this Hackman's hatchet because it cuts through all the competing theories. This five-fingered approach serves many kinds of teams. Like good survivalist gear, it is light enough to carry into the toughest settings.

- Real team
- Compelling direction
- Enabling structure
- Supportive organizational context
- Expert in teamwork coaching

These five bullets can work for team 101 and team 901, but what is missing?

Let me backpedal two minutes.

During the 10 years I played basketball at noon at Clarkson University, bias was everywhere. In general, the engineering faculty I played with expressed a strong bias against my style of "big city B-ball." They played like engineers, in predicable patterns, and cut all the really wild and exciting quick passes at the core of basketball.

Being an exceptionally consistent free throw specialist during the day, I often had the honor of picking my teammates for the noon pickup games, choosing first from the stray set of players waiting there. I deliberately looked beyond size and the engineering class, who often were built more like professional offensive linemen than quick, graceful basketball players. Instead, I would "shock the bias" by picking a few girls to be on my team.

In general, I knew these young women were better shots from the corner and from the key, and by watching them, I knew that these unproven ones were competitive in a good pent-up way.

These college girls, some engineers themselves, were just waiting to take on most of the middle-aged engineering faculty out there at noon. Although some of the Clarkson faculty and researchers would prove, again and again, to be quite decent ball players and some were mighty strong going to the baseline and under the boards for their size—overall, for 10 years, they were consistently unable to keep up with my girls. The final scores proved this in a way even male empiricists wished to deny.

Basketball is merciless this way: speed, agility, persistence, and pent-up aggression count. Time after time, the defeated opposing teams let us stay on the court all noon hour and then some.

We would often win five or six pickup games in a row. As if in replay, we'd be beating the new contestants by 5 points in an 11-point pickup game even before some of the senior folks had tied their shoelaces!

Luckily, I had to teach a class every Monday, Wednesday, and Friday at 1:30, 2:30, and 3:30; otherwise, the other players never would have gotten a chance to roam the courts. It was a very good hour for us spent running full court. We dominated for the better part of a decade.

Such is the bias of men in action. The same pattern can be seen in the history of most professional sports until the 1980s.

Lately, I have been enjoying all the female Olympians from countries such as Turkey and Australia, athletes who are excelling in this new swift century. In the evenings, I spend time reading about historic exceptions that are just now coming to light, having been repressed until this new generation got us thinking. I began to see how teams empower men and women, boys and girls, the old and the newly aspiring.

Scott Bedbury, who advised Nike on these mounting social changes in his fine book *A New Brand World*, can take some credit for expanding Nike's global marketplace by a factor of 2 when he convinced them that this pent-up interest in sports existed in women. Suddenly, sometime in the 1980s, women needed sports gear ranging from bras and socks to refined high-performance shoes.

Of Redheads and Unexpected Victories

This next example is one for the history books.

On September 9, 2012, the *New York Times* printed a story by Howard Beck about Coach Wilbur Surface and his 1936 All American Red Heads basketball team. The story of these folks is coming to light now because they are being inducted into the Basketball Hall of Fame in Springfield, Massachusetts, the result of hard work by one man, Molina. You see, Molina was faithful to the tales of his grandmother about these Red Head players, and one picture she had in her attic proved it.

It turns out that his grandmother was one of the 65 players inducted—65 women at once!

The Red Heads once won 96 games in 96 days, and most of the time they beat the rural men they played against. The surprise result was that the Red Heads would move on, and the men had to stay in the town after their humbling defeat!

The strategy was to hit the new town hard and once. Leaving the town for the new contestants was easy; gaining enough fame when constantly on the road was a bit harder.

The Red Heads finally got their night while I was writing this book, the same time the Hall of Fame was being headlined by "real" greats such as Reggie Miller, Don Nelson, and Jamaal Wilkes.

Nonetheless, the point of my story is they had a real coach, a real team, and some amazing supporting facilitators on and off the court—like all great teams. What lagged behind was cultural recognition of what made them great. (Perhaps in a few years, the story of these Red Heads will be told as a major motion picture starring Scarlett Johansson.)

Let's keep this bias in perspective. This all occurred in the 1930s—about 60 years before the prime-time coverage of the WNBA. This all came down about 36 years before the political rules that allow female play (Title IX). And it all happened a good many years before I did the same rural basketball trick in Potsdam, New York with the Clarkson crew.

According to Howard Beck and the *Times*, "Years ago, Molina discovered a black and white photograph in his grandmother's attic in Glastonbury, Connecticut. It featured his grandmother, Bernice Gondeck Molina, and several other women, the 1934 women's basketball team for the J. B. Williams Soap factory." After that, he removed the kimono surrounding this idea that girls cannot jump and score.

For the record, Matt Zeysing, the historian of the Basketball Hall of Fame, picks at the edges when he notes that not all of the girls were redheads.

The rest dyed their hair for the season.

Getting Deeper Than Hackett and Harvard

In giving you the list of Hackett's preconditions, and then in reminding you of the special exceptional teams neglected in the past, such as the Red Heads or our opening aside on the Dynamo of Eastern Europe (see the Preamble), we are still mostly scratching surfaces, no matter how nice that feels. We are noticing special teams without yet explaining what makes them meaningful.

Near Future Training Tip

It is our contributions to teams—not just our individual achievements—that get best replicated and extended.

For more leadership insights, visit www.ahcgroup.com

The magic of teams resides in something deeper than statistics. This "something larger" cannot be valued only in terms of individuals, wins, and statistics. Instead it offers a glimpse at a more mature, electric understanding of winning.

To further explore the importance in this point, we next examine the human life cycle of teams in Chapter 2.

In that chapter, we are consciously looking for the spots of sudden rightness when we are matured to enjoy a team. Why? Because there is magic in how we acquire a sense of accomplishment larger than the self.

Why an Aside on Aging

There are many, many good books on teams. But most of them jump us right into the action of teams, without underlining the phases that got them ready to be great as teams. I feared that without fully appreciating how this magic of maturation through teams occurs in a world where infants are born selfish and where new team players are commonplace in their excellence, we would take a wonder for granted and miss the point of it all.

In addition, I feel deeply that we (meaning modern civilization) need to rethink both Freud and Marx in a very out loud way.

Clearly, as we age, we mature way past the imperatives of Freud and Marx, while many corporate and social organizations wrongly keep measuring us by these nineteenth-century individualistic measures.

At the same time, in exploring Cicero's classic on a well-spent life, we explore how and why teams make us suspend our own time clocks, look around in a new way, and enjoy a glimpse at something much larger than ourselves.

To Be Young Forever Is No Fun: Summary

★ What makes this world so severe is an over-reliance on youth and individualism.

★ To be young forever is no fun compared to winning as a team.

★ The way to outline the problems of youth is through teamwork and team building.

★ Teams defy ordinary time by providing something larger than individual motivation and accomplishment.

2

Aging across the Ages

The best armor of old age . . . is a well-spent life preceding it. By this I mean a life employed in the pursuit of useful knowledge, in honorable actions and the practice of virtue, in which he who labors to improve himself from his youth, will in age reap the happiest fruits of them . . . because a conscience bearing witness that our life was well spent, together with the remembrance of past good actions, yields an unspeakable comfort to the soul.

—Cicero, *De Senectute (On a Life Well Spent)*

The Problem Question

What *is* a well-spent life? What does it consist of? And how can teamwork help that life grow through its given stages with grace and force?

I often ask this question at the tail end of the day when my daughter is asleep and my wife is busy tending to her mother's needs. I also ask this question during the long global journeys I take for work as a management consultant. I reread some classics during these long flights and accept the swollen ankles and the dry throat in search of some satisfying thoughts about life.

My answer to this prevailing question is simple:

As we age, our definition of a life that is well spent changes. In addition, as we mature from the swift runner to the great team builder, our definition of group success and our desire to achieve group results dramatically changes and matures for most of us.

The Answer Is Balance and Teamwork

And during this magical maturation process, it is our contributions to teams—not just our individual achievements—that get best replicated and extended.

Although standard Western philosophy and our tool chest of classics often seem to celebrate singular individuals who provide intrigue and insight, "the real life of success" (as another coach put it) is more likely a narrative that celebrates the group, the team, and the competition, not just the self, the owners, and the supremely advantaged.

Now, at age 57, I reassess my life from this perspective of how teams informed my maturing. This worked nothing short of wonders in my case.

My friends across four decades, and from college and high school, can recall the flamboyant and arrogant youthful player I was. It was the magic of teams that made me into what many others now call a group leader. The transformation I write about here I experienced firsthand, and it is in the act of writing that many of these nuances and insights about teamwork and aging became clearer in my own life story.

I now can see how aging works best to ready us—universally—for teams. This discovery of the social capital in groups helps us see more clearly how society and business click. This also helps me see why my earlier books about social response capitalism boil down to telling the history of contemporary industrial society as a grand readjustment to new ways of winning. For when we discover social capital, we become more free and less individualistic in how we compete.

Defining a Well-Spent Life through Teams

As I stated previously, the way we each define a well-spent life evolves as we age. But the recurrent and commanding role of teams throughout life's various stages is well worth exploring here.

Although the fundamental elements within the definition of aging never change, we know that each person's life story is as unique as a fingerprint. Still, when we experience the magic in teams from which individuals gain wisdom, we experience something that is actually more universal than unique.

I now claim that what enables this magic in teams involves the strange but common crucible that forges good teams. Over most lifetimes, the experience of being on a good team—or as Williams James noted, "a séance of the group"—transforms us into a larger setting of the self.

We become what the famed poet and philosopher Ralph Waldo Emerson called "delegated actors in fate." I am using these quotes from famous authors to suggest that teamwork proves commonplace and recurrent in most of our life stories. Teamwork forms the vital sap of maturation. (See Chapter 6 for explanation.)

Next time on a long train ride in a foreign country, try this: rather than talking to fellow travelers about work, religion, or politics, confide in the teams you loved—and doors will open to you.

The Transformative Energy in Teams

The transformative energy in teams allows proper aging—the maturation process that peaks in wisdom. Meanwhile, this process also prepares us to accept the phases of aging in our life. After we cocoon as individuals, we emerge with extended wings in teams, larger than if we were merely ourselves.

I know this a bold claim to make—so bold that I even surprise myself in doing so. This is especially true given the fact that until recently, I had always neglected to make something of this groupthink in teams as I told my life story.

I feel deeply now that this ability to refine our acknowledgment of teams will help us outsmart the foolishness we exhibit during our overdependence on youth and individualism earlier in life. And if we can capture more of this magic as it happens in teams, we can acquire some new grounds for hope in the near future.

Where Do We Go from Here?

The central focus of this first part of the book, then, can now be summed up for emphasis with the following three points:

1. **Aging is a process during which we realize our achievements come from teams, from our culture, and from our times.** Aging alone is depressing, compressed, and for most philosophies, well, kind of a downer. However, in the context of teams, it can and often does become magical. This magical realism in teams is more than a literary motif.

2. **When we realize this, we get a glimpse of the value that teams provide**—one that lasts longer and looms larger than our own beings. This is the kind of jump into action that Sigmund Freud and Karl Marx completely missed. This is the jump that extends our wings.

3. **Herein, we transcend our own time on Earth without actually leaving our lives.** How else can we explain that cathartic effect we experience during all those weekends watching our favorite teams?

In this way, teamwork is closer to existential joy than formal religion; however, these higher facts of human aspiration in teams bring us closer to greatness than most organized events.

Although many in ancient times found this higher order of their self in pilgrimages or ritual process, modern-day humans seem to achieve a similar high by following or joining teams—teams that can involve anything from commerce to exploration to the military to mere gaming.

Therefore, although much of Western philosophy since Elizabethan England underlines individual success, real life as we now see it tends to celebrate how these individuals have flourished in teams.

Defining the Aging Process through Teamwork

I now see the aging process itself as a series of action-packed reality checks that remind the individual how best to deliver his or her value to teams—"as if fate itself is one large set of external signals." This is a phrase from one of my high school coaches that has always stuck with me, despite the passing of four decades. It stuck because it aligns the individual ego's impulses and urges to fit or fight the current historical setting. Those who win their share come to understand this or suffer the downward spirals of egotism and self-importance. Throughout human history, the so-called lucky ones were those who could envision the game of life involving these kinds of challenges and choices—and nothing more.

I see now that the opening quote from Cicero comes quite close to describing what is commonly known as wisdom through aging.

In fact, much literature about wisdom focuses on bearing witness to aging. It's about reflecting on how we learn to do more with less in life. The existentialists were right, to some extent: we are thrown into this world, and we must fight to find our lasting balance. And Cicero is more correct: we are born with a need to spend well what we are given. One's life is the ultimate transaction.

A Well-Spent Life Is a Primal Right

Another way to articulate this primal right is in reverse: by spending our lives on well-built teams, we build around ourselves a reputation and a set of relationships that live beyond the self's desire for fierce individualism. This is the opposite of the Macho Paradox, which results in increasing isolation over time.

Those who excel beyond this paradox live long, fruitful, team-based lives.

Here is my premise:

Throughout our history, human beings—despite all our foolishness and power—have aspired to age well. Teamwork seizes this opportunity, and does so with some intelligent guarantees. One reliable way to age well is to invest in the smoothness of teams. In fact, this is our primal right.

This is also where great teams aspire and triumph. It is why great teams such as the Dynamo can triumph even in times of extreme totalitarianism and abject poverty. And once we recognize this primal right, something else magical can happen: despite poverty and disadvantage, we can be elected to be part of a very important team, the very games upon which civilizations are based.

When you read Cicero, you can see that his work is absolutely saturated with this grand assumption of a primal right, a right deeper than freedom itself: the right, from birth, to live well in groups from birth to death.

For example, when I was growing up poor on Long Island, from ages 10 to 18, I felt evidence of this truth often by simply walking to the local basketball courts and playing with teams. All I needed were sneakers, a T-shirt, and shorts, and soon enough, I could move with speed along the lives of at least 10 others in action.

The manner in which Cicero gives us this certainty "to be in the game of life" is what makes his book such a wonderful gift. He informs us, persuades us, and delights us on topics as difficult as the approach of death. The end of games, he notes, prepares us for getting ready for the next game . . . and the next . . . until we are well spent and ready to exist in the inn of life.

Cicero's work is about building the armor to be in love with aging; it's about swimming through life, as if you knew that your arrival at the golden pond of old age were a guaranteed result of a good life.

Near Future Training Tip

By spending our lives on well-built teams, we build around ourselves a reputation, and a set of relationships that live beyond the self's desire for fierce individualism.

For more leadership insights, visit www.ahcgroup.com

Life and Teamwork

Cicero wants to share something universal to all our lives, not only the privileged. He guides us in being a part of society, in being team players both recognized and golden. Like a grandmother telling wisdom-filled stories after a holiday dinner, Cicero wants all of us—not just the bigmouths who know aesthetics and the favored sons who, over time, come to know power—to have a good and memorable time encountering his text.

And as such, he poses the question: What makes the words ageless?

In other words, what characteristics enabled me to convert both my physical and psychological body into a kind of word body that stays suspended in the air, far longer than Michael Jordan in his double-pump fade-away championship NBA jump shots? Of course, this is a complex question.

Cicero is suggesting in his own way that *your life* is the thing. Without much hubris—and certainly with a kind of humble immediacy—Cicero assures us that we have the right to take our lives seriously, even if we are not heroes, even if we were not born special. In this way, he is the author who prompted me to think about the right to write about what's ordinary in the magic of teams.

A Basic Goodness in Cicero and in Teamwork

For those who need a bit of background, Cicero was a formidable Roman politician, a successful attorney, and an orator whose speeches to the Roman Senate resonated with me even though they had been written centuries earlier. Yet we realize something else in reading *De Senectute*—something deeper than these surface credentials: above all, Cicero was a principled thinker. Part of living a well-spent life, then, involves following through on our chosen principles.

So what is a principled thinker? According to Cicero, it is someone who, early in life, guesses that the world of events will always be swifter and more severe than his or her best thoughts and therefore decides to take life seriously. This means pursuing "useful knowledge" and "honorable actions" so that one has a chance of remembering things past with some sense of comfort.

When a dentist uses knowledge to spare patients mouth or temple pain, when a taxi driver conveys thousands safely on their way for years on end, when a carpenter finishes a beautiful house that lasts—these are lives well spent.

Cicero is examining something more basic than social achievement, recognized accomplishment, and rewarded effort, the things that make most histories monumental in their bias. He reminds us that principles are internal and earned—and, at best, *personal*. In a way, principles allow us to spend our lives balancing the external forces of fate with the internal hopes of freedom.

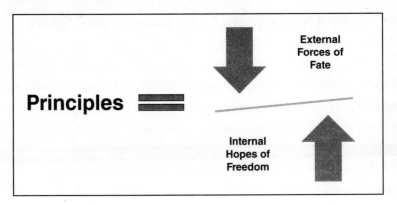

How Teams Help Us Reach beyond the Intellectual

We find something in Cicero much more substantial than Socrates's notion that "an unexamined life is not worth living." Socrates's advice is for something I see as a kind of heroics in thinkers; it's not the fundamental pragmatism of doers and team players.

In contrast to a Socratic dialogue, Cicero developed a sense of the end from the start. He knows each game—each life—will end, so he's designed principles to help us enjoy the game as we play it. And the emotional intelligence required to do so requires that we make some real breakouts. Over time we break away from our narrowing occupation with individual needs and we grow beyond simple individualism.

This sense of an ending is what allows some principles to bloom, mature, and outlast the shedding away of the physical self. Cicero's work is about a pragmatic readiness for the end of life. It's similar to what we do when we engage in estate planning or risk mitigation; however, Cicero does it to ready us for each day in life. He warns us that all competition will end at some point, so we might as well play right or not at all.

Why Modern Life Is So Severe and Swift

We see a contrast in Cicero when we watch how tragic or sudden so many athletes' lives seem after retirement. In these cases, we need to ask: "Why, in contrast, has modern life become so swift and so severe?" Again, I suggest it has a lot to do with our tendency to overemphasize individualism and youth.

When Marcel Proust and other poets in prose confront aging, they often go back to the classic beginning for all of us: the sense of the self in the world. Perhaps all of us know that the world can be mean, fierce, and inflammatory unless we take principled actions. We learn this from life itself, not from, say, reading Shakespeare. It is this kind of learning that Cicero craves to share.

Ironically, Cicero created his masterpiece well before modern learning, and perhaps without a full sense of the entire majesty of the life cycle. Freud and the explosive field of modern neuroscience have taught us that we are sentient beings who experience life's shades and good times, from day 1.

On the other hand, Cicero misses most of this first phase of the self (from birth to the early twenties)—despite the fact that it is an important, magical, and psychologically rich origin phase of the self. Like the world's best attorneys, pragmatic philosophers often undervalue this mystical beginning, yet it is a time during which we become our essential selves in largely proverbial ways.

It is often from birth to age 20 that we first learn how best to fit in teams or not.

In defining a well-spent life that is both principled and modern, then, we must acknowledge the consequence and power of the years from birth to youth in shaping the eventual personality.

The Question of Questions

In his grand finale of Chapter 23 on Cicero's class, he asks this question of questions, from the other end of life:

> Do you imagine, that even I (for as I am an Old Man, I must talk a little of myself), I say, that I would have undertaken such hazardous attempts, and undergone such fatigues by day, such toils by night, at home and abroad, if I had supposed the glory of my actions must terminate with my life, and all my sense of it end with my being here?

Clearly, toward the end of life, Cicero placed more value on achievement than on youthful exploration or childlike discoveries. Just like Freud misses the rich varied value in teams, the great Cicero misses the great beginning in all of us.

When she first heard my voice in the delivery room, my daughter looked at me—straight on, as if she knew the voice and all of its warm intentions. The book *The Language Instinct* now proves that that's possible. The MIT scientists who wrote the book have documented that we are hardwired for understanding and human communication three months before birth!

Babies can see, hear, think, contemplate, draw inferences from patterns and from repetitive gestures, and have fun in the act. These are the essential elements of superb team play, especially the rapid pattern recognition and the joy in repetition.

Yet emotional intelligence—part of what enables us to function well in team settings—is not typically produced through training but through experiences.

Many of us learn this sharing of responsibilities in early teams. It is about getting the solutions in motion, rather than thinking through the problems, you might say.

Indeed, this experiential learning creates trust and builds relationships. As the team members work through problems, they clarify their shared vision and develop a sense of trust in each other by learning how to communicate effectively within the group and how to best work through the situation as a group.

In this way, teamwork becomes the primary creator of value and meaning in our lives.

In short, a well-spent life is not only about aging. All of us are given some special tools from the start that allow us to inspect our lives and grow into team play.

Near Future Training Tip

 As team members work through their problems, they clarify their shared vision and develop a sense of trust in each other by learning how to communicate effectively within and how to best work through the situation as a group.

For more leadership insights, visit www.ahcgroup.com

The Middle Years

In many ways, *De Senectute* relates most to the middle years, where the holy mess of personal growth resides. From the teen years to the beginning of old age, we are aspiring upward while at the same time remaining animal, grounded, able to procreate and to make major drives of ambition, for personal growth requires innovation, intensity, energy, mistakes, and the communication of meaning.

We also choose our battles more wisely as we age.

But many of us still have plenty of body energy to waste during the middle years, plenty of public masks and personalities based on extras to try out, you might say. We are unwitting in this waste much of the time, but it is a part of our journey at this point in our lives. Here is what Cicero says about this holy middle mess:

For I am not at all uneasy that I came into, and have so far passed my course in this world; because I have so lived in it, that I have reason to believe, I have been of some use to it; and when the close comes, I shall quit life as I would an inn, and not a real home.

There is wisdom in viewing life as a solid journey spent well. When we exit the inns of our mistakes with some calm and satisfaction, we arrive at a well-spent life. Furthermore, if we provide some good use in the process, we attain more social power. Those who get past their middle years with such a feeling of usefulness have the most desirable and favorable attributes. There is now scientific evidence to suggest that the ability to feel at home in teams is an important part of learning what leads to longevity, as well as productivity.

The Long Finale

The best portions of Cicero's book are the middle pages (from Chapters 10 to 19). This is where he answers his peers' four objections to old age and ends with a frontal assault on fears and worries about the approach of death.

He does this by confirming his feelings about the premature death of his own son. Strangely, Cicero doesn't show much remorse; this is mostly because he has lived up to his principles. He weighs the trauma from the perspective of his long finale and asks his wife to do the same. I am not saying these middle passages are masterful or mystical. They simply matter.

According to Cicero, those whose lives are well spent are more sanguine when the end comes, because they have the satisfaction of having seen the end from the start to the eventual end. As long as they ran the race with principle, goodwill, and good cheer, they have won. Competitive sports helped convey the same set of conclusions in my life.

No matter how the scoreboard read or what the final record was at the end of the season—whether winning or playing as the underdog—a team provides the chance to be a part of something larger than individual achievement. It gives us all the opportunity to find our place in a group of people with shared beliefs and goals and to stand for a greater purpose.

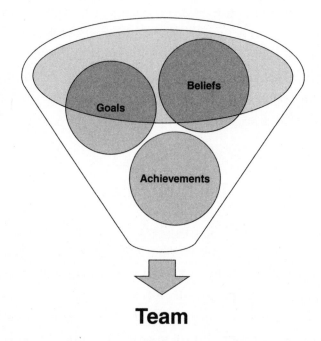

Team

Source: Designed by AHC Group Corporate Affiliates Director Marti Simmons

The Dynamo team gave a nation hope and pride even in the gravest of times. They have the best record in the league at the moment and have the support of fans who will defend the team's honor against any opponent, no matter how grave the odds. Teams give a sense of belonging, a feeling of being a part of something, no matter how big or small your role in it is.

Cicero again:

> We ought all to be content with the time and portion
> assigned us. No man expects of any one actor on the theatre
> that he should perform all the parts of the piece himself: one
> role only is committed to him, and whatever that be, if he acts
> it well, he is applauded. In the same manner, it is not the part
> of a wise man to desire to be busy in these scenes to the last
> plaudit. A short term may be long enough to live it well and
> honorably; and if you hold it longer, when past the first
> stages, you ought no more to grieve that they are over, than
> the husbandman repines that the spring is past, and the
> summer heat upon us, or after these, the more sickly autumn.

Notice the emphasis on being applauded, as we are when we
play the game well. And notice how so much of what Cicero says is
about accepting the fundamental timing in the teams we find in
life and in life itself. Herein rests the very essence of humanity.

Yet in our fascination with the glitter of youth and rapid
ascent, modern man and woman miss this simmer into satisfaction.

But now that I am at middle age myself, this view of the long
farewell makes good sense to me. It strikes me as a more stoic way
of saying, as Walt Whitman did, "Did you know that old age can
come with equal grace, force, and fascination?"

I must confess, I neglected the power of this insight from
Cicero the first few times I read the book. I did this in my
blindness called youth.

Crazy Aging

Our generation outlives those from classical times by two to four
decades. So what are we to make of that? Can we remain team
players in the great last segment of our lives?

A wonderful book called *Crazy Age*, by an 80-year-old British writer, starts with a brilliant definition of why she likes her ragged, overworn sweater and would not want any of her family or friends to replace it.

Although this supreme and carefully written book doesn't accept all the satisfactions that Cicero sees in extreme aging, it does echo—from a modern, sophisticated point of view—many of the things I've chosen to emphasize in this chapter.

There is something crazy about advanced age. As one becomes a senior, a "senator" of the neighborhood, the things in society that really matter become clearer. As our bodies lessen, our longing to be an active part of teams can grow. That, after all, is the definition of a *senator*: "an old wise man or woman." And that is what we find in the arts, in diplomatic circles, and in the many great rural traditions in regard to the elderly.

Rampant individualism and the exaggerated celebrations of youth are tempered through team play. Recently, I reread the anthropologist Victor Turner's classics, *The Ritual Process* and his sequel *Dramas, Rituals, and Celebrations* from this point of view: in all eras, aging is team play at its best, from youthful pilgrimages to end-of-life funeral processions.

All cultures require this adjustment from youth.

By looking through the eyes of Cicero, and then by filtering my thoughts through the scientific experiences of modern research into the neurological sciences, I can sum up productive aging and that well-spent halo by citing four higher facts about aging:

1. **Persistence pays.** It's better to defy your doctor's numbers than to become a victim of too many prescriptions.

   In other words, persistence in teams may broaden dividends beyond all measures. Those who live the longest in industrial societies often have the greater gifts of remaining engaged in teams, social clicks, and sometimes historic larger communities setting the terms and logic of the near future.

2. **You simply do not deal with people you know to be dishonest.** Take them off your teams. Do not allow them on your team, and do not join their teams. They will waste your life. Avoid these negative folks like the plague.

   Cicero wants us to live long, well-spent lives by avoiding this most wasteful path. When we are talented in teams, we can avoid rampant dishonesty and fulfill a coherent set of plans.

3. **You must be a giver as much as a taker.** This involves a sense of play, not just reason-based allocations of your time. Although visiting teammates in the hospital, travelling to them, or knowing and caring about their families may not directly add to your bottom line, it is the stuff that makes real teams. The great team players bring that play into all of life's ups and downs.

   You must learn to jump into the team beyond the measures of the self. Herein resides Cicero's insight into how common the greats in humanity can be. They know how to benefit from the great wager called life by giving even more than they take.

4. **Remember that expert intelligence comes at a cost and that you must earn wisdom, not inherit it.** By earning the status of a wise team player, you have arrived in a well-spent life. It is seldom, in the end, about financial wealth. It is about the currency of bringing value into teams and social value remains the key.

This sums up the Ciceronian way. This is not exactly the same as the Roman way, as Cicero offers a more peaceful and more generous way to winning in which you do not always need to win the current game.

Another thing that makes Cicero's 90-page book great is that it taught me some of these higher facts when I was still extremely young.

Life can be full of grace, force, and fascination, especially if we prepare to find it weekly in teams.

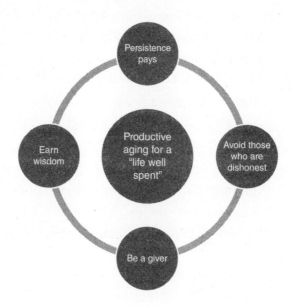

A Concluding Tale on Aging and Teams

Let's end this reflection with a positive example from ancient Indian tales, a tale by the Zuni: "Swift-Runner and the Trickster Tarantula."

This eight-page master story has been brought back to life by Dee Brown in his retelling of this classic Zuni legend. You may recall this gifted writer; his *Bury My Heart at Wounded Knee* has sold more than 5 million copies since its release in 1970. For the fine book collectors who cherish the Folio Society, Dee Brown reassembled a set of classic Native American tales over the past few years, offering us a chance to read three dozen great tales.

The folklore I here present to you from the Zuni offers us a concluding short tale about how high-performing teams (a village, in fact, in this tale) offer a wronged individual (the Swift-Runner) many avenues to resolution and success.

Like so many raw and great folktales, this story's value resides in its rapid twists and turns and in how well it captures a shared actionable understanding of human nature. I sum it up for your convenience, hoping you track down the actual artful eight pages to cherish and to reread to your teammates.

The tale begins a long time ago when there is only one Tarantula on Earth. This giant Tarantula was as large as a man and lived in a cave near the base of Thunder Mountain.

Around sunrise almost every day—in this recurrently beautiful morning in most great folktales—a handsome young man runs by. The Swift-Runner has done this many times before, and each time he is noticed by our Tarantula. This young man is exceedingly beautiful, wearing a headband of many colors, a fantastic belt of horn-bells, and warrior training clothing of reds, white, and greens. The Tarantula is naturally envious of the young man and spends time plotting how to obtain Swift-Runner's costume through trickery.

Swift-Runner is the young man's Zuni name, and he is studying to become a priest like his father. That's why his costume was designed for sacred dances, as well as for preparation to be a warrior. And to keep himself strong for these dances, he runs around the mountain base before prayers.

Upon taking a few steps out of his den one pivotal morning, the Tarantula hears the horn-bells coming again closer. He asks Swift-Runner to run near. The boy impatiently pauses, breathing hard but readying to be polite as trained. The Tarantula notes how he admires the boy's costume and regrets that he—the boy—cannot see how well he looks as he runs by so bright each morning before prayer.

"Why not take your clothes off in a pile by me, and I'll do the same, and then we'll switch the clothing so you can see what you look like." (You can imagine Sandusky doing the same again and again, or one of the priests of the recent past who uses his position in the teams of a church to lure and hurt rather than to preach. This Zuni tale is about the many kinds of praying, where youth collides with aging, and where the dark for a while can outshine even the swift.)

The boy suggests they hurry up, because he does not want to be late for morning prayers. So they take off their clothes right then and there, and exchange them in seconds. The boy says: "Step back a bit further, so I can really see what you see when I run by," and the Tarantula does slowly step back, then in a second, he slides back down his hole.

The Tarantula has tricked the jubilant boy.

A few sentences describe the weight in the boy as he travels back to his homestead, where the village is the same, but he is not. The boy back in the village asks the Falcon for help. But when the Falcon goes for the Tarantula for the handsome leggings, the embroidered shirt, and the necklaces worth 50 times the norm, all he can bring back from the clever Tarantula is the tattered headdress—as the dark Tarantula is clever and forewarned. A Kingfisher and an Eagle had already tried to secure some justice for the boy, but both the Kingfisher and the Eagle had completely failed.

Troubled, the boy next bears his open soul before the elders in his village, who say he should tell his tale to the gods. This ascent toward the just is similar to governance reviews in firms, with the scrutiny more severe at each level and the intensification of consequence felt in this tale.

On his way up the mountain, the Swift-Runner is surprised to find the grandmother of the gods plump and angered. In the folio edition, there is a wonderful image of the grandmother, as both fierce judge and helpful aid, both informed experience and aspiring hope. I smile at this step in the pursuit of change in a large team, as you never know when the grandmother will emerge to remind the youth of his folly.

She really laces into him, nonetheless, underlining his stupidity and indicating how silly he was to trust a Tarantula in the first place! I always love this part of classic Indian tales, because as you know we are reading for redemption. In each classic tale, you also get the clear lesson to avoid being a knucklehead next time.

The boy persists as he knows he is rightly wronged and is told by her how to proceed upward, where he is surprised again by the gods. The gods are not giants, but little somewhat inattentive beasts—or so they seem at the time to the boy—as they give him two clay toys to place by the mouth of the Tarantula's den the next morning before dawn. There is very little explanation of the whys and hows, as they are also testing the boy's trust in them.

He does this—you are getting a sense that the best governed teams have plenty of avenues for redemption and correction—and he begins his redemption by telling the best warriors of his fine village that he needs them on his team, that he really needs them, and he needs them tomorrow morning. Without hesitation and with a sense of service and nobility, they bring their sharpened bows and arrows. The team is working; the wrong will be corrected.

The next morning the clay toys of the gods have become, magically, a frisky deer and a lovely antelope running near the dry mouth of the Tarantula's den. They play a bigger role than the coaches suggested they could.

When the Tarantula comes out, he has at last met his match, as these godlike animals are as swift and clever as he. The warriors aim with glee—they breathe in like generations before them, aim, shoot, and succeed—and shoot him, causing a massive explosion that brought the clothes back to the boy and parts of the

Tarantula to Mexico, South America, and as far away as Taranto, Italy. This again is the magic of teams. The resolution just happens, sometimes in incredible ways.

Dee Brown concludes, with the eloquence his fame allows: "Some say that Taranto took its name from the tarantulas, some say the tarantulas took their name form Taranto, but everybody knows that the wild dance known as the tarantella was invented by Tarantula, the trickster of Thunder Mountain, in the land of the Zuni."

I find this tale a perfect anecdote to what goes wrong at the once-great teams of Penn State or the Tour de France.

Often when I enter a corrupt or badly tainted situation in corporate teams, I keep this young proud Swift-Runner in mind. It helps me turn toward the team for help against the many taller tarantulas among us.

Aging across the Ages: Summary

★ As we age, our definition of a well-spent life changes. Our contributions to teams get replicated and extended during this process.

★ Aging is a process where we realize our achievements come from teams, our culture, and our times. Realizing this gives us a glimpse of a value in teams longer and larger than our own beings: it gives us a higher level of freedom and fate.

★ Cicero's work lasts across the ages due to his universal commonness. This is how we appreciate teams: they are universal and common.

★ Teams that recur with principles noticed across decades are those known as legacy teams or teams of great consequence.

★ As we age, we learn that persistence pays dividends. As we age, life requires zeal and the ability to self-motivate. In the end, value is social not only financial.

What Makes This Century Swift?

3

Team Coherence

Readjusting Your Gaze

realize the aside on aging in Chapter 2 may have startled you. Most do not expect books about change, business, and leadership to be so focused on aging.

But I felt after rereading many books and stories about teams that we needed to create a life-cycle framework around this growing field of human endeavor. In some ways, our near-future rests in our ability to mobilize and balance teams with less bias and more result.

As the world becomes a web of 7 billion citizens—each of whom are constantly seeking food, energy, and shelter—we need to reinvent the notion of shared actionable understanding around the power and magic of teams.

This means readjusting your gaze from individualistic greed to group good and moving from a celebration of youth for youth's sake to a celebration of matured and seasoned sense of shared social capital.

Near Future Training Tip

 Readjust your gaze from individualistic greed to group good, and from a celebration of youth for youth's sake to a matured and seasoned sense of shared social capital.

For more leadership insights, visit www.ahcgroup.com

We Crave Acceptance

Teams make the most sense—and are perceived as legacy teams of great social consequence—when we see them outside and above any single season of play.

Most people, not just business leaders or owners, crave this form of social acceptance. In the end it is not about the current scores and victors but rather about the overall team's impact. When we witness that, we say the team has coherence. Coherence is the very core of what we are calling a new way of winning.

To achieve a sense of this coherence in action, this chapter will explore the dynamics I felt and witnessed during the four years of advising Shaw Industries, a Warren Buffett maker of flooring in Dalton, Georgia.

It is difficult to capture team coherence in a snapshot: you know it when you see it in motion, but it often comes from surprising and delightful mixes and moments within teams.

Furthermore, it is harder to describe in action than to see it in action. Thus, what follows is a sustained analog to the higher arguments of St. Francis of Assisi to help the business reader see these higher facts of team coherence in action.

Although the previous chapter on aging should have helped us better understand the maturation process at the heart of teamwork, this case study on Shaw Industries dramatizes what we crave when we want team coherence in our lives.

Humans are social animals that crave acceptance even more than victory. And we are animals best understood when in group play.

The Problem at Hand

Now we can readjust your gaze and look a bit longer and deeper at the magic of teams. We'll do this here by connecting the principles of St. Francis to the successes of Georgia's Shaw Industries, a Fortune 500 maker of carpet and flooring, and the eighteenth largest user of truck fleets for distribution in America.

First, a higher fact:

Stories and principles in business, as in society, are always more compelling than numbers and metrics.

In fact, there is some basic brain science of perception that suggests coherence is inherently a synthesis in action rather than a set of distinct measureable events. We celebrate coherence far more deeply than measures. And herein lies our first significant challenge in defining the coherence in teams.

Every executive, athlete, and team player is measured, and then remeasured in this swift world.

Our individual performance is gauged from day one each week; we are trained then reevaluated, given different tests along the way, and tested again against team-based and often well-articulated results.

This is the new Mobius strip that embraces all departments and modern teams. This measurement-intensive world of globalized human resources, at first, seems to require that we be measured ceaselessly.

A Step Back

In the medieval era—often now referred to as the Dark Ages—humans centered themselves on prayer without ceasing. St. Francis was one of the first to break from this mold, in a sense, by activating and transforming lives instead of thoughts. His work was about the piety we can find in teams of brothers and sisters, not the dogmatic measures of the church itself.

We see sharp contrast in the modern global corporate mansions, the top 300 largest firms that I have called World Inc. companies. All these Fortune 500 companies plus smaller aspiring firms are dominated by measurement: since W. Edward Deming and Juran, all success is measured success, and all play is based on individual metrics and personal goals.

As all the management books note, "What gets measured gets done."

Yet Shaw's story reminds us of something higher, something more classic and ancient about human accomplishment and drive in teams. For measurement has a profound and recurring team-deadening aspect, something we will refer to as the Tinker Bell syndrome.

The Tinker Bell Effect

In the gym where I work out almost every morning when I'm home, I say hello to the former chief executive officer (CEO) of several large gyms in Texas. She is a recurrent type in the modern gym and the modern office. I have nicknamed her Tinker Bell because she is this tiny, happy pistol of a gym coach who flies among many of us, encouraging us and aligning us to our higher expectations.

Most of my colleagues now happily accept that term of endearment as does Tinker herself. What I say in the next pages is not so much about the Tinker in my life but about the trend you know she represents in your firm and in your gyms.

Tinker reads more books about business than I do and is probably more trained in classical management theory and practice than most of my team. And she comes to my local events with an informed intensity that I can see she brought daily to her prior business.

Like her fictive namesake from *Peter Pan*, she uncovers our memory of youth, sifting through what's possible with our aging bodies, clinging to what's best left in our past versus what remains within our grasp. She has a remarkable ability to remember what our past varsity college and high school sports were. Like all great coaches, she can remind us in a second of our better selves.

Well, the Tinker Bells in modern corporate human resources departments have sometimes flown way into the wild side of human ambition. They have inhaled a kind of fairy dust that leads them to expect everyone to become an all-star. I say this deliberately, as I've seen it in automaking, the chemical industry, and most often in the petrochemical sector—all master planners of their universe.

But we must acknowledge that although the many machines measuring our muscles or our corporate output have our best performances in mind, an all-star like LeBron James has a 1 in 10 million body type; and although we share, in part, a set of genes with him, ours do not execute as well as his does.

This performance gap between the expected measure and reality creates a predicament in which we never really win when it comes to our individual expectations, nor do we ever really feel relaxed or in the zone in the presence of our bosses. That's the syndrome, one that produces a serious and recurrent problem: we respect our teammates, but we resist them if they happen to be measured well before us.

Overmeasuring emphasizes individuals over team performance as a whole and breaks down the shared actionable understanding that creates a great team.

The Syndrome Writ Large

Using these ceaseless measures, our handlers tinker with our best plans to make sure we keep up not with the average but with the exceptional.

We forget our best intentions in the heat of weekly measures, and then Tinker rings loud bells when our results do not measure up to our expected or predicted achievements.

As with the vast universe of instant replays common in modern sports, we can measure corporate variances against the prior year to hundredths of a degree. The machines do not forget, nor does the swift click of the information retrievers. All past successes become today's heightened expectations, recreating a kind of repetitive motion illness to our expectations when expressed ceaselessly over years. Why else would so many well-paid executives otherwise aspire to retire when they reach 58 or 59, my current age?

But the cause for this apparent drop in achievement might be due to the fact that we slept on the wrong side of a new mattress last night or because the quality of the last meal out was subpar.

Unfortunately, this less-than-ideal performance context does not really concern those who measure. I have found that this quest for documented performance can become a syndrome under the following four conditions:

1. **When the current team is not ready for the big leagues,** as is the case in most start-ups. Although they may have good systems, they likely haven't yet developed all angles in terms of distribution and marketing channels.

2. **When the players don't really know their new bosses,** because the merger occurred less than a year ago, and management reshuffling has made the bosses even less visible and less known.

3. **When products have reached commodity or mature status.** In most cases, this is the point at which the business strategy is no longer about price, quality, and innovation in any competitive sense. Rather, it has become about ways to hurt a competitor or to recapture small amounts of market

share. Think here about Walmart's pressures on its suppliers or the legendary fights between Coke and Pepsi.

4. **When the market is weak and not willing to support endless hype.**

Some say these four conditions describe most regional economies after World War II.

Yet the reliance on excessive measurement prevails. This Tinker Bell syndrome is a serious problem, begetting much knucklehead behavior in modern teams. And it leads us to question how this kind of excessive competitive measurement prevents us from helping those we love make the team.

We can see this through a series of short storylines—stories that have become like fables in most midsized to Fortune 1000 firms. And although you can change the names to protect the innocent, the presence of a Tinker Bell, and her recurrent interventions, is what keeps too many of us up at night.

In my view of this swift and severe world, this is all for the wrong reasons.

People perform better in teams when that kind of quantitative pressure is lessened, when there is simply not so much focus on measuring. In this scenario, the best moves are done with zeal and not measurement, and the most lasting teams are based on informed loyalty more so than measurement.

Although the best teams, like the Celtics, celebrate statistical results on rare occasions, they are *always* looking for the next win. The increase in potential exists first and foremost in their shared actionable understanding of the challenges before them, and this lust for potential proves that their smoothness goes deeper than sheer statistical victory.

A great coach or a great captain has the ability to size us up in action and remind us when measurement has distracted us from our true goals and potential. True team integrity—the kind you see in the Celtics or Navy SEAL Special Ops—offers us a unified focus on team success that goes further than what can be measured. All exceptional team performances reach this condition beyond individual measurement.

Our next story about a $5 billion-a-year maker of carpet and flooring illustrates my earlier points by establishing a strong contrast to Tinker Bell–run firms.

Near Future Training Tip

 True team integrity—the kind you see in the Celtics or Navy SEAL Special Ops—offers us a unified focus on team success that goes further than what can be measured.

For more leadership insights, visit www.ahcgroup.com

St. Francis and the Southern Boys at Shaw Industries

I've always gravitated to the stories about St. Francis.

Even as a child, I felt a force that brought me to his kind of storytelling—a set of lasting and colorful tales about friends, fellow travelers, and teams. Most important, I loved that these stories illustrated a set of higher facts about life and how an aspiring self fits or proves a misfit in society.

I often read, studied, and reread his work during high school, college, and graduate school—usually as an act of mindfulness after finishing some large multiyear set of tasks. Then, as an adult, I visited the Basilica of St. Francis of Assisi in Italy. Like the works of Benjamin Franklin that cultivated the business side of me in society, the book by St. Francis kindled my desire for more in life.

I never found reading St. Francis difficult; instead, I find his book in four distinct parts a joy and a stage for many surprises.

This book is richer than its reputation. Over the past 30 years, Shaw Industries has been run with these kinds of higher facts and storylines clear and foremost in the minds of its 6,000-plus carpet makers. In retrospect, I realize I was preparing to work for Shaw several decades before I knew they existed.

The License to Believe Matters More Than Measures

I have found through my experience in working with them that Shaw is a firm based on principles and storylines more so than measures and explicit orders.

When I first parked my car at this Christian value–based manufacturer, I noticed that some of the cars' bumper stickers quoted the scriptures. I soon learned that many of the staff e-mails—particularly those sent by the clerical staff but also some by senior management—included epigrams from the Bible beneath the signature.

I knew from the moment I arrived that it differed greatly from most firms worth more than $5 billion in sales.

I became a top advisor at Shaw rather rapidly in the years after my book *World Inc.* came out. I sometimes spoke before hundreds of Shaw's top performers, but I always came back to run a 22-person council for Shaw's top four executives. Although very much the only one in the room with a strong New York accent, I was comfortable there. My principle-based consulting practice resonated with Shaw's employees, even though they had told me from the start that they seldom brought outsiders in.

For nearly four years, my actions at Shaw served as a practice field to test out and further refine the principles I first wrote about in my book, *Doing More with Less: The New Way to Wealth.*

In the next sections, I wish to take a larger leap into the feel of the Shaw teams with which I worked. They each support this analog to the works of St. Francis in spirit and in detail, without needing to quote scripture or passage.

Getting Back to St. Francis

There were a dozen good reasons that a poor boy like me would respect St. Francis's classic book, *The Little Flowers*. He was a wordsmith and not afraid to argue persuasively. He gamed a complex system of wealth to reach a set of better essences about faith, hope, and loyalty. Later in life, using Benjamin Franklin as a model, I would write a book describing this art of competitive frugality. But in the decades before that, I often regrouped by rereading St. Francis after setbacks.

But what I see now—at age 57—in St. Francis is his fantastic understanding of teams. No one ever taught me that.

He had a vivid collection of special friends, who wove tales about him as a foundational figure in the early church. He was, at times, as tough as a Navy SEAL in his fasts and fantasies and as fastidious as a chief financial officer (CFO) as he ran his early operations. But could his principles be applied to carpet making?

Here is an example from Chapter VIII of *The Little Flowers*, where St. Francis explains to Brother Leo what things are "perfect joy." I remembered this passage when I first met Shaw's chief operating officer (COO) Hal Long, the executive champion through whom we reported. Hal's methodical inquiry into his flock often involved direct messaging mixed with this St. Francis kind of rhetoric of inversion. As a change agent and quality revolution engineer, Hal frequently entertained the vision that things in business are not always as they appear to be. Here is the St. Francis passage from more than 700 years before:

> One day in winter, as St. Francis was going with Brother Leo from Perugia to St. Mary of the Angels, and was suffering greatly from the cold, he called to Brother Leo, who was walking before him, and said to him: "O Brother Leo, if the Friars Minor had the gift of preaching so as to convert all infidels to the faith of Christ, write that this would not be perfect joy."

> Now when this manner of discourse lasted for the space of two miles, Brother Leo wondered much within himself, and, questioning the saint, he said:

> "Father, I pray teach me where is perfect joy."

> Saint Francis answered:

> "If, when we shall arrive at St. Mary of the Angels, all drenched with rain and trembling with cold, all covered with mud and exhausted from hunger; if, when we knock a the convent-gate, the porter should come angrily and ask us who we are; if, after we have told him, 'we are two of the breathren', he should answer angrily, 'What ye say I not the truth; ye are but two imposters going about to deceive the world, and take away the alms of the poor; begonen I say';

> "If then he refuse to open to us, and leave us outside, exposed to the snow and the rain, suffering from cold and hunger till nightfall—then, if we accept such injustice, such cruelty and such contempt with patience, without being ruffled and without murmuring, believing with humility and charity that the porter really knows us, and that it is God who maketh him speak thus against us, write down, O Brother Leo, that this is perfect joy." . . .

And now, brother, listen to the conclusion. Above all the graces and all the gifts . . . is the grace of overcoming oneself, and accepting willingly, out of love for Christ, all suffering, injury, discomfort and contempt.

Hal Long was expert at telling these tales of rejection, reversal, and reward.

Telling these tales about business being deliberately different than it first appears requires a steady hand and a generous soul.

Hal could never have been as encouraging as he was if all he did was rely on past measures. Instead, he was always widening the moat of positive reputation around his firm. Although he was fierce when the team failed him, this is common in all great coaches. And this reaction proved quite rare; it was something I witnessed only twice in four years of service.

Overall, Hal was firm in his expectations—and he expected team results, not individual achievements, to be acknowledged. He held weekly staff meetings, raising the bar and reversing the easy.

Getting Deeper in Shaw and into St. Francis

St. Francis was one of my guiding lights.

During my fifties, I began to see the grace behind his force, a mystical certainty that outlasts the false correctness in modern life and in modern measured ways.

His concluding 18 entries in his classic, *The Little Flowers*, which are attributed to the notable sayings of Brother Giles, contained a universe of shared actionable understanding. I found that Shaw's CEO, Vance Bell, practiced most of these 18 guiding principles with grace and force.

The passages, for example, "Of vices and virtues," "Of faith," "Of sloth," and "Of contempt of temporal things" seem to be the operational principles of some firms for which I've worked—firms based on service to others. Although I do not examine in a literary textual sense what's amazing about each of these sections, what follows shouts out the key principles relevant to modern teams.

The Coachable: Not the Perfect

In rereading these passages today—and after working for Shaw and hundreds of other firms—I remain stunned by the eloquence of St. Francis's vivid argumentation. Like Hal Long, there is a form of certainty and contrast in his words that is rare in ancient writing. Take, for example, this passage, which I believe conveys the point that every player is coachable:

> Nevertheless, let no man, how sinful ever he be, despair, so long as he liveth, of the infinite mercy of God; . . . there is no man in this world so wicked and so sinful but God can convert him, and adorn him with singular graces and many gifts of virtue.

This faith in people's coachability is stronger at Shaw than the usual corporate dream about people's measured perfectability. In this way, they have outperformed their competitors, companies such as Interface and Mohawk, during many rough years. They've done so by putting their faith in coachable hires, rather than individualist—but not always loyal—high performers.

I remember confronting Hal when I discovered that one of their key profit and loss leaders was pressing for something unnecessary. He was doing so because of his resentment about having not been made one of the "big four" after running a unit in foreign lands. Hal sat back, looked out the window, and said: "Bruce, do you still find him coachable? Because I do." This was his way of saying, despite how difficult this man was being, you had better learn how to work with him, not around him.

It is not rocket science to make carpet; however, it takes a functional contempt of waste to do it at the right price, and it takes a hatred of the harms of sloth to make it strong. Shaw recycles more Nylon 6 than any of its competitors, and it collects the wasted fibers from all competitors to process and remake their industry.

In other words, CEO Vance Bell and COO Hal Long have created a business culture with the values of service, loyalty, and teams—qualities that I believe are far more than individual or excessive personal measures.

Near Future Training Tip

 Invest in coachable hires, rather than individuals that are high performers but perhaps not loyal.

For more leadership insights, visit www.ahcgroup.com

A Caveat about Values

Firms such as Shaw Industries are not my typical corporate affiliate. Those globe-spanning multicultural multinationals have many Tinker Bells in each division, and they view measurement as being as important as profit.

Shaw, on the other hand, became a $5 billion manufacturer with an easily discernible set of Southern values. Most of Shaw's hires come from Georgia or the southern region, and most of its executives are Georgia Tech business students and the like. This goes against much of the thinking behind business success books these days, but it taps into a deeper set of values that defines all great teams.

Before I go on, I must confess one thing: I have not confirmed any of these claims with the top four leaders at Shaw, including Vance Bell, former-quarterback-turned-CEO. Nor have I tested the theories of what makes them tick with COO Hal Long, the Georgia Tech engineer who brought "quality" tools to Shaw in the 1980s and 1990s. However, what I am offering you are my untarnished observations from being Shaw's change agent and aggressive New York–style facilitator for more than 40 months.

When I Came into Shaw

I arrived at Shaw Industries in 2007 and stayed until 2011, as a result of my book *World Inc.* (See www.worldincbook.com for some details they first noticed.) I was hired by a long-term friend Rick Ramirez, who had been brought in from chemical giant Celanese in an effort to bring some of that company's methods and rigor to the demands of sustainability and growth.

When I first met with Rick in the early months of his appointment as a senior executive at Shaw, during December 2007, I looked at Vance and Hal and could tell a few things instantly—as they are not the types of executives who hold back. They wore their preferences and their ideas on their sleeves.

They explained to me that they did not normally invite "outsiders" such as Rick or me; however, they had a sense that their company had potential to operate at a level higher than the one at which it was currently operating. As such, they wanted us to work with their teams.

These men had known each other for a very long time. In fact, Shaw's top four have more than 90 years' combined experience at Shaw; Chief Financial Officer, Ken Jackson was the newest to join the top after serving as their Deloitte top accountant for many years. They were as confident as St. Francis that they could be better. I knew I was fortunate to be working with this company; a more perfect setting for a change agent is rare to find.

The thing about the big four—which also included the CFO and head of marketing and business development Randy

Merritt—is that they were a real team. Each of Hackett's five preconditions was evident to me within a few months of sensing interviews. We also conducted hundreds of leadership engagement hours with the top 50 to make sure our change agenda bettered what they already had.

These top four leaders at Shaw Industries met daily, and each held weekly staff meetings. This was profoundly different than the leadership style under their founder, Mr. Shaw, who—as a founding dictator of sorts—called all the shots. These men were a team in a classic sense like the Beatles. They rocked together for a crucial period of time.

But they often lunched and socialized together as well. I spoke with them about their families and met their kids. I enjoyed their consistently civil and friendly company—while knowing them at the same time as tough decision makers. These folks treated their employees like family members even though they employed thousands. You would often get more attention for a moral shortcoming, such as chewing out an underling, than for a business loss, such as exceeding the norm in travel expenses. They possessed the ongoing values and loyalty that we talked about in the early parts of this book.

Some Results at Shaw

I helped these five men build a quarterly review process we called the Growth and Sustainability Council. This included more than 15 functional heads (with six or seven deputies). The group ranged from the profit and loss people in wood flooring, for example, to the heads of technology, manufacturing, and the better-paying business units. It was a complete well-performing team, and I was the practiced team facilitator with Rick Ramirez.

Five of our biggest wins included:

1. We achieved uniform agreement among hundreds in Shaw's prime carpet brands to add 25 percent recycled content to this top-of-the-temple product. This move eliminated a large waste issue, cut production of product costs, and proved quite appealing to Shaw's prime customers, whose expectations were changing.

2. We extended this notion of top of the temple to other related teams—specifically, to include other characteristics of eco products throughout Shaw Industries.

3. After a voluntary agreement with the Department of Energy, several dozen technical members were able to reduce an energy bill that exceeded $200 million dollars per year by 14 percent. In some years, they were able to achieve nearly 18 percent savings through this journey to lessen team efforts.

4. The Growth and Sustainability Council earned the attention of the CFO, the CEO, the product profit center heads, the comptroller, the information technology (IT) leader, and the human resources staff, and it earned the attention of most of the key product family champions. This offered team coherence and team integrity, a clear line of sight from the top four at Shaw to their key players down the field.

5. The Growth and Sustainability Council took on a key training role. Before we got there, many claimed that Shaw lacked a strategy. The company was gifted with plenty of market presence and real technical skills and assets, but the team's common objectives were not evident or actionable.

Two things led to these five avenues of improvement. First, there was clear and discernible strategic humility in Shaw's top leaders, which is not something I can say that about most Fortune 500 clients. You feel it in the air at Shaw Industries; in everything they accomplished, they rehearsed how it could be made even better without excessive pride or greed.

At the end of a key chapter in *The Little Flowers*, Saint Francis notes:

> Greatly ought a man to fear pride, lest it should give him a sudden thrust, and cause him to fall from the state of grace in which he is; for no man is ever secure from falling, so beset are we by foes; and these foes are the flatteries of . . .

> A man has greater reason to fear being deluded and overcome by his own malice than by any other enemy. It is impossible for a man to attain to any divine grace or virtue, or to preserve therein, without holy fear.

Again, I never asked Vance Bell or Hal Long directly a single thing about Holy Fear or about St. Francis. But I saw it, as others have, in most decisions they made, and in how they act.

After all, it was not my job as a management consultant to ask them about St. Francis. But the way they saw their teams was similar to St. Francis in a direct and fantastic way. They did not litter their plans with hubris, tragic loss, pride of sudden thrusts, or psychic delusions like we find at companies such as Enron or Adelphi. This firm had a kind of strategic humility at its core. People came to the meetings on time, with strong opinions and stronger actions.

How Does This Humility Relate to St. Francis?

You cannot get team play without clear principles in many corporate circumstances. Another way to say this: most modern firms suffer from individualism and from the pride of youth because they lack a clear storyline that connects their heritage and best ideals with the current state of play in the market. I did not witness this common failure mode in any of Shaw's divisions or teams.

It is only with a clear set of higher facts that you can earn the attention of change, because most individual incentives in firms are people-based and thereby people-limited. Vance and Hal and their CFO Ken Jackson saw it another way.

Near Future Training Tip

It is only with a clear set of higher facts that you can earn the attention of change, since most individual incentives in firms are people based and thereby people limited.

For more leadership insights, visit www.ahcgroup.com

How I See It after Readjusting My Gaze

St. Francis's writings remain my mantra to get at something different that abounds in a firm like Shaw Industries.

St. Francis's boldness caught my eye when I was 12 through his statements like: **"For all that is written of God is but as the lisping prattle of a mother to her babe."** Sure he was a poetic teller of tall tales, I thought. However, this inspired in me as I aged a form of respect that made me return to his masterpiece again until I could understand the balance of argument in this four-part 58-chapter book.

St. Francis's arguments are well organized; the parts add up to a kind of crescendo, and each story is additive in a sense of the way teams achieve coherence from their legacy. Michael Porter is famous for saying strategy is not about perceiving yourself as great. Instead, Strategy—with a capital S—is about running a firm where all activities add up to increase in the profit margin. This takes focus, and it takes the work of good teams.

CODA

During one of my last visits to Dalton, Georgia, I brought my copy of *The Little Flowers* for the long flight home. I remember vividly that this trip was just a few short years before my mother passed away after having a sudden heart attack.

After that visit to Shaw, I was shocked to learn that the primary person who hired me had left the company after about four years to work at Siemens, which posed a much larger challenge. Shaw had not fired this man: he chose to leave the company for a bigger position at a global industrial firm.

I was readjusting my gaze during this week or two. I had produced more than 100 case presentations for Shaw's council and had touched the work lives of hundreds of the staff. I had then taken my mother—in her 80s at the time—up to the Adirondacks for our July 4 summer retreat, along with a copy of St. Francis's *The Little Flowers*. I needed that break, and I had brought the right book for perspective.

My mom's eyes were worsening, at the time, and she talked about a "flower that jumped from its vase" onto the breakfast table. Being always a bit mischievous, I chose to read to my mom Chapter XXI. In this chapter, St. Francis speaks of the miracle of how he tamed the fierce wolf of Gubbio, his equivalent to a jumping flower.

The priceless four-page storyline starts like this:

> At the time when St. Francis was living in the city of Gubbio, a large wolf appeared in the neighborhood, so terrible and so fierce, that he not only devoured other animals, but made a prey of men also; and since he often approached the town, all the people were in great alarm, and used to go about armed, as if going to battle.

The conversation between St. Francis and the wolf is unlikely, again full of reversals of expectations and a real kick of a story. I believe the writer's intention was for us to smile in disbelief upon hearing the tale. St. Francis's focus in this peculiar tale is different from his stories of miracles involving teams; here, he fixes the town's issues alone. My nearly blind mom suspended its articulate unlikeliness and absorbed it as a form of the most pleasant wishful thinking. "Much better than Freud's wishful thinking," she said, as I ended the fourth and last page. Then we enjoyed a long pause together. I did not know how little time I had left with my mom at that point.

Near Future Training Tip

Change requires force, grace, and fascination.

For more leadership insights, visit www.ahcgroup.com

According to many etchings of this wolf sitting like a trained dog before St. Francis outside of the embattled walls of Gubbio, this wolf in rage calmed down.

People have repeated this story again and again through the ages; they have painted it, etched it, and talked about it day and night. They swear by it, well outside of the confines of Gubbio.

Here is how it ends in the book—St. Francis recommended that the people feed him directly, leaving food outside their doors, and says:

> At last, after two years, he died of old age, and the people of Gubbio mourned his loss greatly; for when they saw him going about so gently amongst them all, he reminded them of the virtue and sanctity of St. Francis.

Change requires force, grace, and fascination. Shaw's top leaders knew that. They allowed me to embellish my work with stories as fantastic, at times, as the best ones in St. Francis's writings. They believed, quite accurately, in themselves, without pride or greed—and they believed in the change agenda they hired me to bring to them. They got their results.

Like life itself, business settings are often full of panic and resolve. A corporate team can be a god-forsaken place where we stand among a wreckage of bad decisions trying to find some new spark among the ashes. Shaw's leaders decided to appease those beasts and to resist Wall Street's wolves by selling to Warren Buffett, who had a way about him that fell in line with their faith in themselves. In the case of Shaw Industries, this appears a blessed decision. Avoid Wall Street; go private, and make carpet.

My mother knew this all instinctively. She framed my readiness, which St. Francis, filled in. The great storytellers of business know this about higher facts, instead of measures, and from time to time, you see it in the best teams in action.

Team Coherence: Summary

★ Today's swift world is characterized by ceaseless measuring, IT intensive and globalized human resources.

★ Some firms remain managed by objectives, run by principles not fierce measures. Such is the case of Warren Buffett's Shaw Industries.

★ St. Francis wrote a classic full of supreme storyline reversals and very clever argumentation on perfect joy and strong faith in values.

★ In today's global, corporate world, what gets measured gets done. However, there is a serious downside to this we call the Tinkerbell syndrome.

4

Team Integrity

Extending Our Wings

The setting is relatively simple: the Boston Celtics play their home games at the TD Garden, a functional building they share with the National Hockey League's Boston Bruins. The goal toward which they strive as a team is equally simple: the Celts have won 17 National Basketball Association (NBA) championships, the most of any NBA franchise.

But what's more impressive and even more important than these wins is the tale of their tall successes. It's a tale that involves a complex team that's composed of a set of players, each of whom is unique. In this way, the Boston Celtics embody the essence of team integrity: something difficult to describe but easy to love—and very easy to enjoy when you spot it in action.

The Tradition

There are some teams, such as the Los Angeles Lakers and the New York Knickerbockers, that are better financed than the Celtics. Their budgets, financed by some of Hollywood's and Manhattan's most famous and wealthy patrons, allow them to sign top players, creating a very deep bench. The ringside seats at their stadiums are reminiscent of where Romans sat at the Colosseum to watch Gladiators.

In contrast, TD Garden has plenty of high-flying cheap seats. That doesn't mean that they do not sell VIP seats. However, it does compel one to notice that a common working-class feel saturates the place, as well as the player's tradition.

Some professional basketball teams, such as the current champion Miami Heat, now have taller and faster players. Even the new finalist—the Oklahoma team—offers glimpses of individual greatness. Their team includes current-season MVP 7-footer Kevin Durant, who can dribble and pass like a point guard even though he towers over most defenders.

Throughout the NBA, there are about 50 super players who can be rightfully compared to the top four Celtic players you will read about in this chapter—and that's my point. What makes the Celtics special is something that has to do more with coherence and integrity than individuals and youth.

It's been said that success is composed of one part natural abilities and one part motivation. Somewhere in this equation is something deeper than individual passion and zeal, something more special than groupthink. It's something that I call team integrity.

I know quoting these two words together is almost countercultural. *Integrity* is normally associated with Western cultural traditions about individuals, not teams. Our myths and biographical books are full of individual achievers who face the great odds of youth and fly into a life of achievement and integrity.

This might be due to the fact that hero worship is easier to grasp in way. Consider the colorful works of American writer Joseph Campbell and his astute, carefully articulated set of recurrent journey steps of the hero. Like Sigmund Freud, Campbell focuses almost exclusively on an individual. And as much as we want to assume that someone can do it all, we know that's not true. We want the hero to win every time, when we know that's not possible.

The Celtics are a team that defies this personification of heroes. And I find that this popular bias for heroic individuals does not capture even half of what makes the Boston Celtics special to many—and noticeable to all.

In contrast to almost all other teams, what Celtic players have is a respect and a shared actionable understanding for the integrity in their team. Every player plays as if he were a delegated actor who's thankful for being a part of this team's deep and ongoing tradition. Sure, every season has its ripped seams and tension between the coach and key players, and every game has its not-yet-predetermined dynamic. Yet game after game after game, you can see in action precisely what I am writing about.

All the *Boston Globe* coverage or news about the Celtics' individual hurts or pains usually proves moot when game time arrives. The transformation is magical. The players arrive ready to extend their wings again. We can immediately witness their team integrity once the action starts. The individuals are smoothest when participating as part of this visible tradition.

I am not only talking here about the large green midceiling hangings that remind the crowd and each player of the conference titles—21, to be exact—and the 17 years at the top of the league:

1957, when I was two,

1959, when I remember attending the first game with my uncles,

1960, when the 1960s began but basketball kept them on top in

1961,

1962,

1963,

1964,

1965, and

1966.

Yes, of course, this was a legendary team with Bill Russell, who some remember more fondly than say Bob Dylan or the Black Panthers of the time.

But it continues, as established in detail by AHC Group Researcher Stephen Gardner, to include:

1968,

1969, and by the time I am at Cornell as an undergraduate, they win again in

1974,

1976, and then they pause. You ask what happened these five years in decline?

I incorporated my firm in

1981, another championship year for the Celtics, then again in

1984, in an almost Orwellian fashion, then again

1985,

1986,

1987 and then that four-year strange and wondrous stream of championship seasons is stopped by some real competitors like Michael Jordan's Chicago Bulls.

But then again, you see the Celtics on top in

2008,

2010, and while they have lost the year (2011) that I am writing this book, I expect the tradition continues well into this new century.

Near Future Training Tip

Success is comprised of one part natural abilities and one part motivation. Somewhere in this equation is something deeper than individual passion and zeal, something more special than group think. It's something that I call "team integrity."

For more leadership insights, visit www.ahcgroup.com

Beyond the Roll Call
and the Team Announced

So how is this "legacy of a team in motion"—this sense of palpable team integrity—transacted?

I have noticed that when you bring a competitor into a setting with other highly competitive people and you remind that person of the high marks and incredible standards his or her forbears achieved, the world becomes less severe and less swift.

The first time I experienced this feeling was at a Lefty Driesell University of Maryland basketball camp in the early 1970s. Lefty paired 17-year-old Mitch Kupchak (now general manager of the Los Angeles Lakers after a distinguished college and pro career) and 16-year-old me with some very serious professional players from the Baltimore Bullets—namely, Kevin Loughery and Earl the Pearl Monroe.

The world slowed down for me that summer; I felt it was my chance to play with the *real teams*. I came away from that experience having never played so well in my life. (I also came away knowing I was not destined to make the pros, a subject worthy of inspection another time.) But my point here is that I passed the basketball equivalent of the 3-minute Navy SEAL drill (which we'll discuss in more detail in the next section) that summer, and it involved access to team integrity training.

Let's call this feeling when you suspend disbelief and dive into team integrity the very *opposite* of simple peer pressure. That is the magic in all of it.

Suspended in this group expectation of the Celtic legacy, I've watched many accomplished players become incredibly more effective upon joining the Celtics over the past 30 years. This is what I mean by team integrity; it betters all.

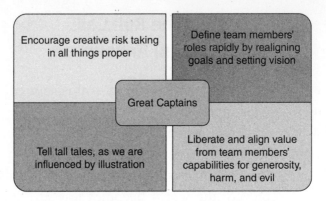

Source: Assembled by AHC Group Staffer Carla Smith.

Parallel Traditions from Soldier to Soldier

The Navy SEALs exploit this atmosphere of competitive alignment during their 3-minute underwater drills. Here, a senior member who has done this drill many times before starts the process. He reminds the new recruits that it is hard to do, but that it is *doable* and that it is honorable. They descend immediately below to kneel on the bottom of a pool. The posture is not threatening for the qualifying SEAL.

Additionally, it puts the "players" in a posture of the tradition, as they know many others have completed this drill before them to qualify. They're also aware that many other water drills have preceded this, like the ocean-side "patience" drills discussed later in this chapter, where you are a part of a larger group. But with the 3-minute drill, you are part of a more elite group—one that's closer to qualifying.

The recruits are then warned that the senior SEAL will be there for the full 3 minutes and will test them further than they expect. If the senior SEAL thinks recruits might be slacking, he will show them they have more in them than they realize.

This is not presented as a threat but instead as part of a longstanding tradition. The senior SEAL is there as a "bug in our ears," as something we get used to during our actions, as these senior members are often talking in their ears from remote locations during actual live actions.

So just like a Boston Celtic has Doc Rivers at the bench barking select orders, the SEALs have the senior. He is there to act like a captain without actually *being* a captain.

Now, some folks have more natural lung capacity than others. However, we can increase our native capacity to hold our breath without panicking through training.

But that is not the point about atmospheres of extreme team integrity. The recruits are able to do together what they have seldom done alone because of the tradition, because they know it *can be done*, and because they are in a group of peers who expect them to complete the test.

A Further Explanation of How the 3-Minute Test Works

Tom Rumsey is a retired Lieutenant Colonel for the US Army Reserves who served in a Special Operations Task force in 2004 in Afghanistan headquartered by the 3rd Special Forces Group. Tom brought my colleague Carla Smith and I into his trust, giving us a framework to understand these special ops teams. He is now a senior executive at GE, a company that has a tradition of hiring ex-military.

Although I spoke to an array of special ops former soldiers who were willing to give me background on their formation of teams, none gave away any information that was secretive or dangerous to the team. The intelligent sources are far more interesting, in the end, than the heroics you see on the SEAL blogs, in movies, or in training tapes now available after the Osama bin Laden kill. Real special ops teams are about the *team*, not the stories or heroics.

Tom gave the best quotable material on this higher set of facts. It's his focus on this—on something GE knows he brings to its teams—that makes him such a valued contributor on this topic. That's why GE hires about 30 ex-military members every year; it's a surefire way to fast-track them into forming effective team-building networks at the firm.

Tom's experience with the coordination and motivation of a military legacy team occurred during his first training set, when he was flying in a group of eight helicopters, with Air Force jets above them and hundreds of infantry on the ground below. As he recalls, "[I suddenly saw that] I was much more involved now than I had ever imagined possible and that everyone around me shared my purpose and my hopes."

The trust was evident in the synchronized movements of all groups participating. All those involved knew that they were willing to take a bullet for those on either side of them and that the feeling was reciprocated; they had a shared trust and vision.

As Tom explains, "It was not simply the reality of the hundreds of men around me forming the large airborne team, or the thousands more on the ground. . . . It was the legacy of the decades before each of us now, of men working and determined toward the unified, common goal; those who were lost and those who achieved great success . . . I saw all of this at once."

This moment of sudden rightness is one way to describe one's initial awareness of team integrity. The legacy of the military is created by every entering soldier who learns the history of the previous members of that same team. It is not just the current military team; rather, it's *decades*—sometimes even cen-turies—of actions beforehand that create a unified perseverance to not let *anyone* down, not the teammates currently before you and not the ones who fought in past history. As Tom said, "You don't want to be the guy who lets the legacy down."

This shows the power that a legacy team has to motivate new members—based on both the current reality and the past team successes and sacrifices. This takes a special degree of team integrity, one where the line of sight from top to bottom, from past to present, from each member of the small team, acts coherently and almost instinctively. You can see now why they are called special ops; their actions involve operations that are conducted in small tight units. They're somewhat like a basketball team, except instead of winning, their mission is to kill.

Why the Celtics Keep Winning

My theory as to why the Celtics can win—even when tired, older, or taxed by travel—is that they have the intangible value called team integrity. It is very different from the kind of individual pride and competitive spirit we find in many athletes and the exceptional dares that youth allows. This matured seasoning of team integrity involves the entire franchise, from the team physician and trainers to the head coaches and franchise owners.

This is what makes the Celtics more fascinating, and the Dynamo team more uplifting. It's what brings more than the simple determinism of weight, speed, vertical jumping, shooting skills, and will into a game. The power in this team includes some folks you might say are the basketball equivalent of "crazy aging"; the general manager, Danny Ainge, is not young, nor is the current amazing coach, Doc Rivers (whose son is already a college star).

And the players you are about to meet—such as Kevin Garnett—are not young either.

The Coach Is the Past Player

Doc, once a very good player himself, fits with the general manager Danny and with the culture of the team like a smooth hand in a well-fitted glove. When you watch them in action, you can see that they share the confidence you find in their players, as well as a strong sense of faith in their team.

You can witness the pride in the tradition and the confidence in their players. It is worth recalling these Hackman elements (see Chapter 1) of a team in the context of the Celtics. In my reading of basketball history—and in my observations as an avid fan who has watched dozens of competing teams—the following five Hackman's hatchet qualities are obviously embedded in the Celtics:

1. The team must be real, not exist in name only.
2. The team must have a compelling direction.
3. The team must have an enabling structure that permits and stimulates team integrity.
4. There must be, from year to year, a supporting organization that brings context and tradition to the current team.
5. Someone or several leaders in the group must be expert in team building and in coaching for teamwork.

We can test this list by applying it to both the team's current players and its ownership structure. And I will pursue this with an awareness of the Celtic's key rivalries: currently, the Los Angeles Lakers, and in the past, the Philadelphia 76ers, San Antonio Spurs, and Detroit Pistons.

First, let's introduce the 2011–2012 team of great integrity.

Embodiment of the Animal
Magnetism of a Great Competitor

One of the first players to join the NBA directly out of high school (thanks to grades and drive), Kevin Garnett just rejoined the Celtics by signing as a free agent in late June 2012 for his eighteenth, nineteenth, and twentieth seasons with the team. This endurance alone is exceptional, and it's what's earned Garnett a spot in the Hall of Fame.

I remember the grace, speed, and incredible outside shooting Garnett exhibited when playing for the Minnesota Timberwolves. But once he became a Celtic, this stunning player developed an inside game, took on a new role as motivator and agitator, and became one of the most consistently performing big men in the league. He is one of my favorite players.

Harvard's great thinker on competition and strategy Michael Porter notes that true strategy involved making sure every activity is a step to increase profit margin and improvement. This is a very important point often missed by folks within corporate teams; these individuals often pursue a technical or a project simply because they *can*.

Kevin Garnett is the type of player who has the discipline to take actions that increase the margin of victory with every single game he plays. This is why we can call his team play strategic. Many refer to this veteran's high basketball IQ. I like to think of it as more specific: each of his activities is designed to improve the play of the overall team.

Paul Pierce: One of the Most Deadly Clutch
Shooters in the Game

What I find fascinating about Paul Pierce is the fact that before the Celtics, no team thought he would be such a critically valuable player.

In fact, Pierce was tenth overall in the 1998 NBA draft. But the integrity of this team allowed him to better himself and the team each year since that historic draft. Most cannot remember the nine players chosen before him that year. By 2008, Pierce led the Celtics to a stirring, six-game victory over the Los Angeles Lakers during the NBA finals. In many ways, the Lakers were faster, more talented, better financed, and more rested. Yet the Celtics came through for the victory—in one way or another—in each game.

Pierce developed some of his most envied skills in the atmosphere of the Celtics. Although a bit slow footed at first, he worked tirelessly to improve his speed, stamina, and shooting on the move. Many commentators have noted how Pierce is at his best as a Celtic—when the game is on the line.

As a Celtic, Pierce is remarkably able to assume the pressures of the moment. His continuity of play is essential during these clutch pivots in a game. Even when the spotlight is focused on another player, my eyes watch Paul if it's a tight moment in a game. You'll often see him making a key steal, a key defensive move, or a key pass. His play is tailored to the situation.

One of my basketball friends, who prefers to remain unknown, said that he hates how announcers talk about how Pierce "dishes out pain" to the opponent at the right moments in a game. My friend says think about this cooking metaphor more closely and apply it to how he actually plays the game. He offers, my friends notes, "more a stew than a stir fry," in that it takes time for the fans to see the flavors and textures to develop in his game. And time is an element that tends to favor his play.

Rajon Rondo

Rajon Rondo has a different set of qualities and tendencies. He is perhaps the most introverted super player I have ever seen; you can almost see him *thinking* his way into the game.

He is a hidden treasure of a player who was even more hidden during the bright start of his play in youth. Drafted twenty-first by the Phoenix Suns in the 2006–2007 season, he was rapidly traded to the Celtics his rookie year. Rondo is no more than 190 pounds at 6 feet, 1 inch, and his fearless drives to the basket reveal a controlling point guard who is completely ambidextrous.

His breakout performance came during the 2009 NBA playoffs, where he helped his team take on the eventual Eastern conference champions, the Orlando Magic, in seven games. Since joining this high-integrity team, he seems, like the others, to better himself each season and is now leading this special Celtic team with players like Garnett, Pierce, and Ray Allen, who has one of the most efficient and the fastest distance shots as a shooting guard in history.

Ray Allen

Despite the fact that Allen retired from the Celtics the season after the one I am writing about, he is a key part of the team's underlying integrity. It will be very interesting to see how the Boston Celtics perform next year without his outside shot. They say Ray Allen has always been an exceptional player, but he needed the Celtic real estate address to become the bona fide legend and Hall of Famer he now is.

After a dozen seasons with Milwaukee and Seattle, Allen found his place with the Celtics—with long-distance shooting that keyed the 2008 championship and that provided a few records as the Celtics strove for another title in 2010.

What else do you say about a player who never appears selfish but, you learn the next day in reading the papers, dropped 40 points on the opponent the night before?

The fifth, sixth, and seventh players on this amazing team alternate depending on time of year, health of the players, and the opposing lineup. And that is part of the magic of team integrity. Somehow Doc Rivers can mix and mesh the players as the season progresses. Yet whomever the starting five are in the lineup, you can see Hackett's five principles in action.

Steve Jobs, the Boston Celtics, and the Beatles

Steve Jobs, in a 2003 *60 Minutes* interview, summed up something that I think is worthy of this book:

> My model for business is the Beatles. They were four guys who kept each other's . . . negative tendencies in check. They balanced each other and [made a total] that was greater than the sum of the parts. That's how I see business: great things in business are never done by one person, they're done by a team of people.

For me, the Celtics embody this principle of the integrity of teams. There are many books about individual integrity. But we're emphasizing team integrity here—a visible and hard-to-achieve wonder.

Many have argued that teams like the Miami Heat, with high-profile players such as LeBron James and Dwyane Wade, will have trouble returning as champions after this year. Like the Lakers, each of the Heat's players are out for themselves—and rather brutish about it in contrast to the Celtics. Although these Hollywood superstars remain exceptional athletes, with skills and abilities you find in one out of 10 million humans, they cannot rebalance themselves in the same way that the Celtics are able to. They cannot balance each other's negativities, as noted by Jobs. So although they offer us fantastic games, runs, and stints, we don't see in them that teamwork of the grander nature that we admire.

Unfortunately, we find those same individual motivations, those that degrade team integrity and unified success, in the corporate world. Individuals work for themselves and not for the team; this scenario comes about when the team coherence, integrity, and team qualities that Hackman's hatchet describes are not present. Financial status drives personal improvements, and the importance of teamwork lessens. In contrast, these individual motivators are often absent in the military world and in many sports teams with great team integrity and leadership. In the military, promotions are based solely on performance for the better of the team. Likewise, sports appointments to starting positions on legacy teams are also based on their abilities to help the team succeed in games.

We'll look more closely at this functional sense of team coherence by discussing some legendary corporate teams in the next chapter.

Team Integrity: Summary

★ The Boston Celtics embody the essence of team integrity. Not to mention they have won the most NBA national championships.

★ The Celtic player has "respect" and "shared actionable understanding."

★ Team integrity betters all players by reminding a good competitor that they are in a group with other serious competitors and that their task is difficult—but possible—to accomplish.

★ The players on a good team—like the Celtics or the Beatles—balance each other's negative tendencies.

A New Kind of Winning

5

Lance Armstrong and the Pleasures of Accomplishment

We have made some bold claims about the value of teams to human life in this short book. So far, we have talked about the magic, the power, and the glory found in teams. At times, we even explored how teams extend our wings, as if all games went upward and outward, no one was ever seriously hurt, and losing was quite different—and luckier—than what everyone else expected.

Part of the fun in being a team player is that even though we know we will stumble and fall during the competition and while fervor fills the chase, we also know we'll get up and try again with some success. But this chapter is not about exploring the powers in persistence or the strange complex of pleasure and pain in endurance. Instead, it looks at the kinds of training and preparation for teams that bring us very difficult but needed life lessons, such as:

- How to play through pain
- How to resist the criminal opportunities inherent in becoming a most valuable player
- How to keep your feet on the ground despite being a member of special teams with special force
- How to outlive uncomfortable appointments, such as being selected for teams that are a bad fit and being chosen for teams you do not want to play on
- How we find, in the end, a pleasure in *accomplishment*, not in youth and individualism alone

This chapter is designed to get us back to Earth, back into the darker side of teams—the place where we struggle to maintain our identity and our productivity. But it's not all bad news. We will take some time at the end of this chapter to reflect on the basic pleasures in group accomplishment.

Let's Start with Some Contrast

Most teams are good for us.

I know they were in my life. Overall, teams have been very good for me, granting me preparation and performance time and the satisfaction of accomplishment. They have taught me the competitive traits to foster and those to avoid.

In addition, the overaccumulated performance of those hundreds of people I have now hired reconfirm this faith in the common goodness of most teams. With few exceptions, most of the performers in my group (www.ahcgroup.com; established in 1981) come from settings where they thrived in teams and they accomplished a lot before accomplishing even more in my teams. In a way, each senior associate in my group was like a Kevin Garnett coming to my Celtic culture.

Perhaps most important, in terms of having faith in our near-future, most of my consulting firm's competitions were fought with fair competition standards front and center. This reality of good governance, and good teams, at the largest companies we serve is not popular in firms today. Yet it has been my experience. Hard, recurrent teamwork pays the bills and accumulates wealth and freedom over time.

And despite all the worry about bad corporate governance and the next Enron, most of the teams that I've facilitated or advised—in the hundreds of management gigs my firm has engaged in over the past 30 years—are enriched by good, solid teamwork. Firms have hired us as management consultants simply to take good teams and make them better and more competitive.

But it is naïve and dangerous to suggest this is always the case. In this vast universe of competitive action, some achieved great success through harm and evil.

The Temptations of Ceaseless Victory

While I was writing this chapter, in October 2012, my mother-in-law's "most favored athlete," Lance Armstrong, suffered a most significant fall from grace. Moreover, the actual teamwork he led was labeled criminal, fraudulent, and intimidating—and now after some time has passed, the entire 20-year tale seems worthy of a racketeering investigation.

I want to use this case to underline the many temptations of ceaseless victory. This has been a part of human folklore since Icarus flew too close to the sun. But the fact that all humans have waxed wings is so easily forgotten during exceptional runs to the top. Some say that only the imagination is real in severe conditions of ultimate competition. I tend now to suggest that only teams are real.

The Fall from Grace

On Wednesday, October 11, 2012, the media was poring over renditions of a 202-page report and thousands of pages of legal documents published and released by the US Anti-Doping Authority. The *New York Times*, my mother-in-law's favorite source, called it "a massive team doping scheme, more extensive than any previously revealed in professional sports history."

This discovery was disturbing to me, enough to shake my confidence for a few days in writing this book.

I regrouped and remembered how excited my mother-in-law was a few years back watching each stage of Armstrong's seventh

Tour de France win. I recalled how she and my wife talked about how incredible it was, this man who had lungs larger than life.

We even recalled that time he had a rider before him crash, and as he veered into a French open field, he tore through the bushes and hedges and the ravines with perfect balance. I heard the same early defense of the great competitor again and again in the YMCA gym I visit each morning.

We had read Armstrong's two autobiographies, and at first I had said, I admired how he knew enough to hire the best sports ghostwriters.

And now, after his stripping of the awards, I asked, "Why would a man need two autobiographies before age 50?" Even Cicero waited until he was in his 60s before referring to his life as well spent.

Then, when the news of the massive network of deceptions came out, I began to recall impressions of the fierce individualism in Armstrong, as if all of his team was there only for him. And I began to see how doping allows this fascination not only with constant victory but with feelings of superhuman youth.

His fall began to take on the shape of the central claim of this book: that competition based on fierce individualism and youthful arrogance is not, in the end, as enduring nor as satisfying as competition as part of teams. The world has become so swift and so severe, that when we let those two pinnacles of hope become too monumental and too central to our expectations it appears even more swift and more severe.

And in recent months, the lawyers in my firm and I had, during leisure times together, wondered aloud why Armstrong chose not to defend himself against those new claims—after he had passed more than 500 professional drug tests during his reign. It seemed curious and indicative of something deeper and still to be unearthed, as in a Greek tragedy.

Here was a storyline where at every turn in the decades of competitions, the story involved dramatic, high stakes, and very visible drama, as well as a web of secrecy and repression.

Suddenly, in mid-October, the darker side of Lance Armstrong was revealed, bringing it all into a whirlwind of suspicion for the general public:

- Twenty-six competitors verified the US Anti-Doping Authority's claims that Armstrong had been doping. They provided vivid detailed confessions. I have looked over the thousands of pages and can tell you it would cost a fortune, in the tens of millions, to file a countersuit.

- Eleven world-class teammates from Armstrong's teams documented how all the doping practices were centered around and for Armstrong. This included new documentation to the *Wall Street Journal* in a letter from Levi Leipheimer, who, for the first time, admitted his own doping in a painfully passionate disclosure.

- Then George Hincapie, Armstrong's closest friend and fellow teammate during each of the seven victories, broke his silence on the matter on October 10, confessing that he was doping with Armstrong and had provided some of the testimony behind the report by investigators.

From a legal perspective, this one-two-three-four punch hit home, especially when it came to Hincapie.

Hincapie is the only rider who was at Armstrong's side for all seven of his Tour de France victories. In the early days, he had retained a lawyer in California, but when he learned this lawyer was an avid fan of Armstrong and a strong supporter of the Livestrong Foundation, Hincapie had his midnight reawakening. As he decided to hire a new lawyer based in Manhattan, Hincapie came forward as the one person who had direct knowledge of the situation during the height of competition. The inner hub of a spinning wheel began to move in reverse.

It is now clear that Hincapie met with federal investigators voluntarily in August 2010, documenting when Armstrong had used blood transfusions, the red blood cell boosters EDO, and large amounts of testosterone, to name a few enhancers.

Coming Back to 2012

The wheels of justice grind more slowly than the pace of an expert cyclist, so things took until recently to go public.

At first it felt like a Greek tragedy, where all the harm was heard about but all the action of the harm was hidden behind the stage.

Friends of Armstrong were still out there. Some were saying he should be allowed to keep his chairmanship at Livestrong Foundation, even if he had to be stripped of the victories he had held in such a ceaseless way.

Armstrong's well-paid lawyer, Tim Herman, for example, as recently as mid-October 2012, criticized the US Anti-Doping Authority actively, reminding those of us thinking about the matter that they used government funds to go on a witch hunt, focusing on a *retired* cyclist, which was a violation of the US Anti-Doping Authority's own rules and due process.

This attorney's artful antics have an ancient ring to me, such as when Roman senators were caught in scandal. They would send friends into the chambers with arguments both vehement and deceptive, meaning the Latin word *vehmentis* in its essence—they were violent and vigorous in their own defense. In retrospect, these artful arguments seem so idle, hopeless, and misdirected.

So, in the wake of vivid and ever-worsening news, as the world began to understand the magnitude of Armstrong's deception and the central role doping played in his career, those who supported him at first began to fade away. In this second stage of recognition, I felt I have seen this pattern before only in great Mafia stories, where the gang leader's parents, children, and friends are seen in a new darker light, seen as intimidated pawns strung along by the leader.

But then, in a later phase of appropriating this news, I began to see this was about the very essence of competition and about how we need teams to keep perspective.

From a corporate governance perspective, we all strive in this field to keep perspective to be alert to wrongdoing. The human desire to be appreciated is overwhelming, and there are conditions when everyone else is willing to go along with a wrong. We recall instances in recent history where the politics of fear allowed the Nazi to reign and where embezzlement seemed a norm. Yet it is harder to see when victory shines so bright.

Here are some of the darkest points of this very dark story of mishandled teamwork:

- The report documented how Armstrong "acted with the help of a small army of enablers, including doping doctors, drug smugglers, and others within and outside the sport and on his own team."

- Dr. Michele Ferrari, Armstrong's Italian doctor, whose name gets tied to the most notorious doping cases in history, received, from 1996 to 2006, more than $1 million in service fees from Armstrong—just like a mobster's well-educated lawyers.

- And again, like in RICO lawsuits, some of those who told the truth against "the man" were punished financially and deliberately. For example, Leipheimer, a long-term teammate, learned from his agent that his normal contract was not renewed; Armstrong's Radio Shack team reportedly told

Leipheimer's agent that they did not appreciate his testimony in federal investigations.

For those who want more on the legal process and the confession history, I suggest you read Juliet Macur's *New York Time*'s pieces, where she documents how "Armstrong's Wall of Silence Fell Rider by Rider." This is often the case in complex strong man cases, where it takes a community of solo confessions to get to the inner core of the team culture.

This report was 164 pages, many of which were punctuated with 850 additional pages of addenda and documentary evidence worthy of a high trial. It was not until the final third of these 164 pages that they then moved in for the kill, noting the evidence made clear that Armstrong had "ultimate control over his own personal drug use" and that "he also dictated its use over the doping culture for his team and the sport at large."

Suddenly, the athlete under the stress of competition began looking like the mobster at the center of the tale. I say this with great hesitation, as I allowed the thought to enter my mind after only abundant evidence. The report continued, "It was not enough that his teammates give maximum effort on the bike, he also required that they adhere to a doping program outlined for them or be replaced."

And herein rests, I would add, the saddest feature of this tale of Lance Armstrong, his true autobiography, for our book about doing more with teams.

You cannot do more with teams in an atmosphere of intimidation, deception, and contract pressures.

You cannot ride into victory more than average with that much weight of secrecy on your mind.

You cannot make friends victims as you claim victory.

This all goes against the magic of teams.

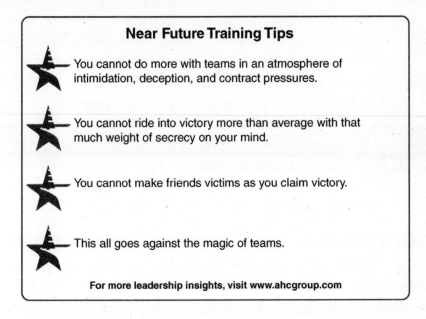

Near Future Training Tips

You cannot do more with teams in an atmosphere of intimidation, deception, and contract pressures.

You cannot ride into victory more than average with that much weight of secrecy on your mind.

You cannot make friends victims as you claim victory.

This all goes against the magic of teams.

For more leadership insights, visit www.ahcgroup.com

To stand out in any team, you become a signal light of the norms to winning. What you eat, what you say, who you date— these are all mimicked, for good reasons.

Apparently, Armstrong wanted it this way. He was not the victim of a doping community; he was the doping kingpin, the originator and its defender, within a small elite networked economically advantaged community of special athletes. It takes a village of people to uncover this kind of haunting truth.

For when horrible things happen to competitive teams, much of it does go back to the person on top of the totem pole. We will end this book by examining the role of captains in keeping exceptional teams together. For now, it is enough to set up Armstrong as the camera-ready example of contrast.

At this point, after rereading the lies in Armstrong's well-written autobiographies and after retracing the steps to discover the depths of the deception, a few things need to be remembered regarding teams. We end this chapter on the darker side of teams with a summary rendition of these few things worth remembering.

Lessons in Deception

Near Future Training Tips

One of the most tragic recurrences in all teams is the willingness to give the victor the benefit of the doubt.

This begins the path of deception.

For more leadership insights, visit www.ahcgroup.com

One of the most tragic recurrences in all teams is the willingness to give the victor the benefit of the doubt. This begins the path of deception.

If a coach needs to bench a superstar, know it is for good reasons. If a referee needs to make an unpopular call, trust it is because he or she saw something not quite right. Overall, there are many systems of governance to ensure fair competition. We all know they are not perfect, but, like changing winds, history forms a kind of spinning and rebalancing wheel so that normal competition can be lively and exciting in our lives.

There is also a kind of deception in mobs. Groupthink is the opposite of true teamwork.

Think about all those who knew for years that they as individuals could not counter Lance Armstrong—how it took 26 world-class cyclists to counterweight his counterfeit. Now this tells us something about popular deceptions. The world is full of dominant views, and one of the most dominant is that the victor gets the benefit of the doubt.

Although most of the press focuses on the special individual achiever, the superstar, we have emphasized how the training inherent in team play is available to most of us.

We called this the pleasure of inclusiveness in the great teams. In sharing shoulder strength, the full team is always stronger than the waxed wings of the superstar.

Near Future Training Tip

In sharing shoulder strength, the full team is always stronger than waxed wings of the superstar.

For more leadership insights, visit www.ahcgroup.com

And although most people in the press place an unrelenting emphasis on winning, we have begun to explore this new kind of winning where the pleasure is in the competitive game itself, in *how* we do our jobs, not only in a positive, measurable result.

I think if others had taught Armstrong between his first and second autobiography the tolerance of losing is mixed with the pleasure of knowing we have tried our best, he would have proved a more dependable competitor.

The great chief executive officers (CEOs), the well-compensated doctors, the best-in-hospital administrators, and the legendary leaders of colleges are not people known to expect constant victory.

They are great competitors because they accept that we cannot always win but find pleasure in the act of competing.

We call this the pleasure of keeping perspective in competitive settings—this forms perhaps the most important ingredient in surviving the stress and trauma of business competition across decades.

Near Future Training Tip

Keeping perspective in competitive settings forms the most important ingredient in surviving the stress and trauma of business competition across decades.

For more leadership insights, visit www.ahcgroup.com

Here at the AHC Group we have designed a number of training cases and modules to deal with super-talented young executives who might become victims of ceaseless victory like Lance Armstrong. It is a key part of our training for the near-future.

Training for Teams, and Training for the Near-Future

Without a doubt, part of what bonds all these good and bad experiences in teams is the pleasure of accomplishment.

There is a deep pleasure in knowing you won fair and square and a deeper pleasure in that you lost with grace or that you helped a team recover its negativities into the positive.

Let's end this chapter, then, on the pleasures of accomplishment, with a little more digging into why teams tick faster and with more fascination than individual egos.

At the start, I mentioned that we added this fifth chapter after the Armstrong explosion hit the news to better explore the dark side of competition, that cliff-hanger kind of experience where things far deeper and more complex than pleasure are at stake. Some of these deeper emotions involve a fear of failure, the need to serve, and most surprisingly, the knowledge that we need to learn how to lose—for after all, we have a short time on Earth to learn many things.

Sigmund Freud once tried to reduce human complexity into a ratio of pain to pleasure. We end this book with examples and concepts that show how the dynamics of teams involve patterns of human emotion far more complex than a ratio of simple pleasure (for example, winning) to pain (for example, losing).

In its place, we now explore how victory and fame, individual achievement, and bouts of youthful joy are merely surface indicators of how public identity takes shape. We then propose that in most human cases, teamwork takes this feeling of public identity, something different than simple self-worth, into new orbits for the competitive.

The Fantasy of Ceaseless Victory

There are too many celebratory books about team achievement. Just like there are too many books making the successful business icon look like a faultless king.

They note how teams extend our wings—as if all games went upward and outward, no one was ever seriously hurt, and losing was quite different—and luckier—than what everyone else expected.

This, again, is part of the magic of teams. But those teams that remain magical also know how to avoid simple deception and face the facts of loss. In fact, after I lost my father early in life (at age three), I remember burning off most of my anger through teams. They could absorb so much of this personal angst through positive efforts. I thereby avoided the easier outlet of abusing drugs or hanging out with the worst kind of kids.

Beyond the Myth of the Ceaseless Victor

Most of us know that an undefeated season is extremely rare, and many of us are prepared to never experience that oceanic feeling of always being on top.

In fact, many of us are satisfied with simply trying our best and achieve deep satisfaction when we win "more than our share."

So when we talk about the common event of loss in competition, we talk about how teams teach us much about being human and hopeful in the face of loss. These lessons can and should be taught early in life.

Are we teaching our future MBAs the right view on winning? Do we give them reasons to resist striving for constant victor status? In contrast, I believe I have been a relentless competitor because of my early appropriation and appreciation of defeat and loss.

Is the Ability to Lose Innate?

I have been thinking about these claims for the past three years, as I've watched my 16-year-old daughter set for her varsity volleyball team. In the many super teams she has competed against, and in the many exposures she had to truly great athletes in her North East traveling team, I can say with some confidence that she has already learned how to get more from a game than a feeling of defeat.

I think it may prove true that young women have a greater ability to cohere as teams and a faster bonding set of habits and that there is something in their biology and cultivated instincts that absorbs the sting of defeat faster than what is seen in boys. You seldom see anyone sulk on my daughter's teams for more than 10 minutes, whereas I've had teammates ruin a season after one or two bad games at the start of the season.

Yet some boys learn early the value of preparing for defeat. And I am beginning to wonder if learning to accept defeat is a key feature of the preparation of teams.

Part of the fun in being a team player is that during the competition we know we will stumble and fall, get up, and try again, with some success. We call this the pleasure of persistence, the sheer thrill of striving.

There is solid scientific and neurological research available to support this. If you Google "emotional intelligence," you'll see that you can discover through teamwork the skills related to success—more so than IQ does. Some of these attributes are seen in teams; some, exclusively in individuals. But overall the ability to motivate one's self, the ability to demonstrate zeal, and the evidence of persistence are what separate the values in doing anything of consequence. Please note that most of these involve a large portion of defeat along the way.

When we enroll an executive in my firm's leadership training program, either in our 27-year-old ongoing Achieving Results workshops twice a year or in our new **Training for the Near-Future** freestanding curriculum, we try to teach the "water walkers of the near-future" the following five lessons involved in teamwork:

1. How to play through pain
2. How to resist the criminal opportunities inherent in becoming a most valuable player (avoiding the Lance Armstrong path to victory)
3. How to keep your feet on the ground despite being a member of special teams with special force
4. How to outlive uncomfortable appointments, such as being selected for teams that are a bad fit and being chosen for teams you do not want to play on
5. How we find, in the end, a pleasure in *accomplishment*, not in youth and individualism alone

This chapter was designed to get us back to Earth, back into the darker side of teams, where we struggle to maintain our identity and our productivity in the worst of team situations.

What Enables a Team Leader to Be Inclusive and Tactful?

In noting the drama and the horror of someone like Lance Armstrong and his distorted and extended team, we begin to think about the links between good corporate teams and good sports teams. In today's competitive world we do not expect a CEO or a military general to be as gruff as Armstrong when, back in 2001 in a Nike commercial, he made money lying: "What am I on? I'm on my bike, busting my ass six hours a day. What are you on?"

Clearly, today's world expects a different, more authentic team leader.

For example, many of the best diplomats in corporate life whom I've worked with got plenty of their training in sports and vice versa. I have always believed that the goodness in teams transfers lessons to all segments of our life: from relationships to revenue generation, from reputation to respect.

For these reasons, I am beginning to redesign some of our training units at the AHC Group to pursue this lesson about needing to confront and then avoid the dark side in seeking ceaseless victories.

Here is how I think it can be done. It involves these features and traits needed for successful near-future leadership.

We sum them up in Appendix B, based on some traits the World Business Council for Sustainable Development (WBCSD) notes as mission-critical for apt business and executive training in our shared future. Here, let us mention the five of them in abbreviated form so that you can see how it could help future Lance Armstrongs avoid falling from grace:

1. Understand the broader context of competition.
2. Manage complexity, by coping with uncertainty, and the ability to tolerate defeat or loss.
3. Utilize systems thinking in a fashion that builds teams.
4. Work beyond normal and limiting boundaries so as to increase global access and inclusiveness in products and processes.
5. Enable innovation past existing laws and rules.

These are, of course, simplified by my team in action.

For example, although most of this chapter was written by many for the WBCSD, we have adapted it into training casework to make it live in people's mind and become embedded in their practices. This was done for my group by three people: Steve Willis, the former global environmental officer of Whirlpool; Ken Strassner, our senior associate, who was Kimberly Clark's vice president in charge of energy, environment, scientific studies (its government relations), and sustainability, and who was involved in the WBCSD debates and helped us refocus and make more useful the findings from their many global surveys; and Gerald Bresnick, the executive champion of the effort for my group.

I think it pays to talk about the multiple competencies it takes to refine the listing of the five traits noted. For example, Gerald was Hess's vice president in charge of environment, social responsibility, and philanthropy. What enabled him to have such a wide and broad view of the complexities facing a global oil company? His PhD in biology represents his ability to understand technical nuance and illustrates his diagnostic rigor. His Harvard MBA underscores a second set of competencies in economics, business, and policy.

But it was his years of action and decision making that enabled him, Ken, and Steve to be such great mentors when they train junior and very promising younger executives in our assignments.

In the end, our near-future training programs are about demonstrating this new kind of winning for our new globalized world. Will it help prevent future massive cases of fraud from happening? Will it allow teams to better realign their money, people, and rules of self-governance? Will it help us catch up to the many issues of sustainable food, energy, and water now before the companies that make our food, energy, and water?

Only time will tell. But the revelation of a case like Lance Armstrong adds some urgency to our desire to understand the science and common sense of teams a bit better in our own lives.

So before we conclude, a few more considerations on the dark side of things.

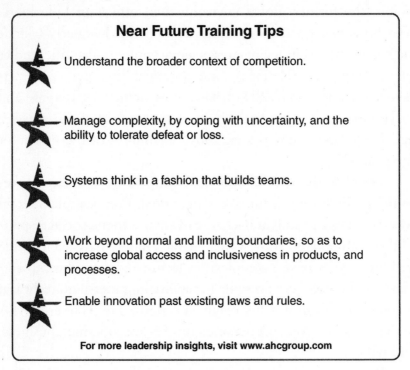

Near Future Training Tips

Understand the broader context of competition.

Manage complexity, by coping with uncertainty, and the ability to tolerate defeat or loss.

Systems think in a fashion that builds teams.

Work beyond normal and limiting boundaries, so as to increase global access and inclusiveness in products, and processes.

Enable innovation past existing laws and rules.

For more leadership insights, visit www.ahcgroup.com

An Ancient Worry

We feel very fortunate that we've been asked to develop this kind of training by a set of vice presidents and clients whom we have served as consultants or as corporate affiliates. But now, they are away from the office more. Their good fortune to be appointed vice presidents has, at times, stripped them of the ability and time to mentor their successors adequately.

Yet because of their sense of the permanence of teams, they wish to restore this missing juice to the future of the game.

Being aware of your good fortune is a supreme blessing—and, at times, an abrupt curse. This is another way of saying that when you are on great teams, you still worry about how long the run to fame and glory might last.

Why is this? Why are we subject to this ancient and recurrent worry, and why do we wonder, even while still in the light of victory, whether we will fight yet another day near the top of our league?

During my four years as a varsity basketball player in high school, for example, I understood all too well the tale of Icarus, whose waxed wings flew too close to the sun. In my case, it was a series of knee injuries that brought me down.

Even when I was outmaneuvering the double-teaming of my baseline moves, I knew that the fade away would not always work—and I developed some trust in the fact that my team would rebound or would give me another chance if my last try was a miss.

Reliance on a team's fortitude and preparedness is a special trust and a source of great satisfaction. Yet there are a number of tests we need to withstand before we find our right team, that is, before we swim in the right pond.

Near Future Training Tip

 Reliance on a team's fortitude and preparedness is a special trust, and a source of great satisfaction.

For more leadership insights, visit www.ahcgroup.com

Playing Through the Pain

The horrible first truth is that not everyone makes the team. In fact, most do not. But if you think too much about this kind of pain, you lose your ability to focus on what you need to do to make the team. Some believe that in learning how to make the team, we learn how to be selfish survivors.

However, I do not agree with this harsh, excessively individualist view of competition. For example, I know I made captain of my high school teams—track, soccer, and basketball—whenever I could make those on the team look *better as a group* than they had during tryouts as individuals.

Therefore, my experience tells me that the act of being selected onto the team refines social instincts when coached properly. All chosen players have the chance to improve their talents and diminish their weaknesses, as well as benefit from coaching and working with others in the process.

The problem arises if a player is coached to excess. In this case, the pain of excessive competitiveness is known to create a form of solipsistic behavior a few smart psychologists have called the MVP syndrome. This occurs when an individual loses sight of the team that gave him or her an identity—the group with whom the person worked to produce the fame for which he or she is now known. Eventually, the person begins to place higher values on his or her individual success than on teamwork.

This syndrome afflicts players who were stars in their day—and who then become addicted to the entitlements of their past. For instance, after each game my team won for years, we got free pizzas—all we could eat—for the starting team, the replacements, the cheerleaders, and the coach's families. This was superb, as I was poor, and the guys would thank me as if I was paying for all this. This did not, however, contribute to my MVP complex as much as the cheerleaders' and my fellow players' families' attention.

In his book *The Macho Paradox*, one Chicago psychiatrist does a wonderfully detailed job of documenting why MVPs gone corporate often find themselves in tight spots, frequently guilty of favoritism, sexism, and even white-collar crimes such as extortion and embezzlement after their individual fame has blinded them of their trust in teams.

The pain of making the team is learning how *not* to fall into the rut of expecting one's glory to continue. It requires that we acknowledge that even individual recognition is brought out—and made possible—by team performance. It pays to learn how to keep your feet on the ground, feeling thankful to the good fortune that brought you the attention, but to be ready to resist any special favors or attention for a past that no longer really exists. As one coach put it to me, "The best players are those who never allow themselves to get too ripe to fail."

Perhaps the best way to outlast this tendency is to realize that there is always a larger league and a set of better players out there, no matter what you've achieved or what rung on a ladder you've just reached.

The Pleasure and Discipline in Preparation Time

In the act of preparing for a team event or in becoming a member of a team, a transformation occurs where team members end their individual associations and create a team identity through sharing with others the experience of that process. Once the team is created, a strong bond is already in place from that preparation and from the obstacles everyone had to overcome to get there.

When joining the military, everyone has a crucible, basic training, which really isn't basic at all and is usually the hardest experience to get through. The crucible is something all members have to overcome to be part of the team. They shave all the soldiers' heads to take away their individual designations and rebuild them as team members, to reshape their identities into a shared identity.

In other words, everyone has a shared experience, through which they earn their way on the team. What makes teams successful is a sense of commonality, shared values, integrity, and commitment to one another. These are all created through experiences as a team, such as going through basic training together: right away, all members of the team have the same crucible because they all got through it.

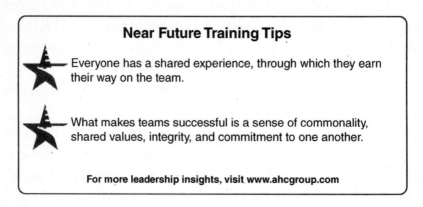

Near Future Training Tips

Everyone has a shared experience, through which they earn their way on the team.

What makes teams successful is a sense of commonality, shared values, integrity, and commitment to one another.

For more leadership insights, visit www.ahcgroup.com

The figure below shows how a group of individuals are brought together to form a team. The lines represent the crucible, like basic training for military teams that each team member must go through to make the team. It unites them under a common experience and binds them together as one coherent group.

The Wisdom in Teams

Peter D. Kramer has written a disciplined and fascinating book about the life of Sigmund Freud for the Eminent Lives biography series titled *Freud: Inventor of the Modern Mind*. About midway through this well-written book, Kramer reflects on the key project Freud launched in his forties, before he achieved world fame, and notes:

> Freud [aimed] to be remembered as a discover of fundamental laws, like Newton's laws of motion, from which the workings of a field of science can be deduced. . . . The notebooks are peppered with scientific looking sketches of neural pathways, the "Project" is largely psychology or philosophy cast imaginatively in the imagery of brain biology.

Although Kramer notes that, as world fame eventually surrounded this superior writer and thinker, he abandoned his "projects" on several occasions, he goes on to say:

> He continued to believe that the fundamental human goal is pleasure, understood as a lack of excitation. Unreleased sexual energy in particular maintained a special role, as a toxic agent. In practical terms, this formulation meant that Freud gave no recognition to positive drives, such as altruism, curiosity, social integration, and enjoyment of competency.

In my way of experiencing the world, herein lies the reasons why Freud ignored both team formation and the satisfaction that teams bring—a viewpoint that, for a long time, succeeded in distracting many people from a life of teamwork. As stated by Kramer:

> The Freudian man, the man of the Project, acts only because he must, on his journey toward inertia. For Freud, intimacy,

self-knowledge, and even awareness were states humans entered "faute de mieux"—the price exacted by reality on creatures born to prefer isolation and ignorance.

In this key insistence of Freud, we find a person who believes that our central drive for pleasure would have us seek not to be perturbed and that the demands of reality always mess up our desire for inaction and forgetting and repression.

In this way, Kramer argues, Freud translated a stream of ancient wisdom teachings into brain biology "and then reasoned forward from the biology to discover the same philosophy, that we are creatures bound to be frustrated, not least by the social universe, in our search for pleasure."

And what a misread of our situation this has become. Sure, Freud's model may explain a bit as to why sociopaths kill innocent bystanders or why neurotics have trouble enjoying a Woody Allen film. But he does represent someone incapable of the passion in teams.

In conclusion, when we look at the tragic fall from grace in someone like Lance Armstrong, we see the cost of an excessive expectation of constant victory. When we consider the radiance and the pleasures of accomplishment in teams, we have set up a contrast worthy of most of us.

6

Freedom and Fate
in Teams

While writing this book in 2012, many of the people to whom I became close during my interviews and research asked me the same question again and again: "So, Bruce, with all of this talk of teams, how do you define a *captain?*"

We have captains in industry, and many groups in corporations are aware of that. We have captains on sports teams, from soccer to basketball to football. And we have captains—or what are called seniors—in most military special force teams, from the Navy SEALs to the other forces.

My definition of a *captain* is someone who can recognize rapidly the key capabilities of his or her team members. Captains treat their team members with a kind of fierce immediacy, and they achieve team coherence and team integrity in the process.

Near Future Training Tips

 My definition of a captain is someone who can recognize the key capabilities of their team members.

 Captains treat their team members with a kind of fierce immediacy, and they achieve team coherence and team integrity in the process.

For more leadership insights, visit www.ahcgroup.com

The Best Captains

Captains emerge in many situations. There are team sports captains on the field and the floor, Navy SEAL seniors who command their own units, profit and loss presidents of business units, and working heads of lower-level business teams. One unifying feature of captains is their ability to quickly and accurately assess their team members' capability and talents—and to figure out how they affect the group as a whole.

The best captains rapidly recognize three kinds of capacities in people:

1. The capacity for generosity
2. The capacity for harm
3. The capacity for evil

And they do it as time moves swiftly forward.

Game Time of Teams Is Forever Moving Forward

In every kind of team, there are recurrent patterns of generosity, harm, and evil in teams. The captain must recognize this with acumen.

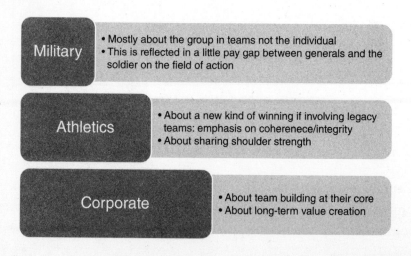

Military
- Mostly about the group in teams not the individual
- This is reflected in a little pay gap between generals and the soldier on the field of action

Athletics
- About a new kind of winning if involving legacy teams: emphasis on coherenece/integrity
- About sharing shoulder strength

Corporate
- About team building at their core
- About long-term value creation

The best and most effective teams balance the negatives in each of us, making a stronger and better core.

Consider what the late renowned Apple chief executive officer (CEO) Steve Jobs said about the Beatles: "They are the best example of a team since they balanced out each other's negativities across decades."

One can of course immediately recognize some positives in the capacity for generosity. It's evident in the way a talented point guard like Rajon Rondo of the Boston Celtics sees up the court and makes everyone else on his team look better after one of his precision high-speed passes. Granted, his pull-up also gives him the ability to harm; but for Rondo, much depends on the capacity for generosity, and his coaches know that.

You see the same capacity for generosity in an innovation champion like Gary Yezbick of home components manufacturer Masco. In the six years I've watched Gary in our biannual two-day long workshops, he is consistently growing the value of our exchange through acts of focused generosity.

I believe this feel good ability to generate momentum cannot be undervalued when forming teams.

The Capacity for Harm

Capacity for harm is also immediately visible in sports teams. From the hockey defenseman who settles a score to the baseball player who dislodges the ball from the catcher's glove while sliding home, we see the tendency to do harm in athletics almost as something *necessary*. In fact, if the grace of generosity is a smoothing factor, the force of harm matters just as much—if not more—in highly competitive settings. Harm is even a net *good* in some instances: if you can knock your opponents off their game, you may enjoy beneficial returns. The act of doing harm is either positive or negative depending on the circumstances and the characteristics needed at the moment for achievement. I am amazed at this point in life how much MBA training avoids mention of this fundamental aspect of success.

In my last book, *Doing More with Less*, I described the type of knucklehead behavior whereby individuals believe their desires are more important than those of the team. These people therefore create harm by failing to work toward the unified team goal and may even create evil by inflicting damage on others in pursuit of their selfish ways.

We often see this kind of knucklehead behavior on the sidelines of sports games as well, when fans cheer wrongly or unfairly. Unlike those knuckleheads, however, well-known athletes today show an extreme, almost military-like, focus on their team's mission.

The Capacity for Evil

This surely is one of the most difficult traits in rapid human action to detect early and swiftly. That is why it takes so long to uncover cheating by athletes such as Lance Armstrong, to learn what's wrong in a firm from the top at firms such as Enron, Adelphie and the investors such as Bernie Madoff. It was difficult to discover what was happening inside Joe Paterno's empire, for example.

The capacity to recognize evil is often left up to a very few in a firm or an organization. Yet the captains of all organizations need to recognize and describe this capacity very well.

This year, after watching his superb presentation to my 80 multinational corporate affiliates, I revisited Cornell to interview the veteran board member Robert Swieringa, a former dean of the Cornell Business School and a long-term member of several boards. We spoke about dozens of key accounting and governance issues before firms today.

As I interviewed Robert Swieringa, an 11-year veteran of GE's board of directors, he instantly understood the need for the captains to recognize harm. Swieringa spoke freely about the training he had undergone to detect fraud and embezzlement and the need to take rapid action across the organization against those capable of evil. None of this was specific to GE or a firm, just something generalized in all.

In contrast, this capacity to recognize both harm and evil is something every special ops military veteran is willing to discuss. However, this tendency was a more uncomfortable topic for people who work in not-for-profit settings and most corporations. These are, after all, places where evil is left for the captain to recognize or for the general counsel to settle.

In the corporate world, only a mere 1 to 3 percent of employees in a large business are capable of evil in the form of embezzlement or extortion. This makes it an easy task for captains of industry to reward the rest of the 97 to 99 percent when acts of good behavior occur, thereby creating team coherence. Naïve is the person, however, who believes *no one* is capable of evil. Although the presence of evil is small—and doesn't always destroy a team—it is important to recognize that it *is* there. We are all fortunate there are alert governors like Swieringa at the top of the best firms.

Near Future Training Tips

 Naive is the man however, that believes no one is capable of evil.

 Although the presence of evil is small—and doesn't always destroy a team—it is important to recognize that it is there.

For more leadership insights, visit www.ahcgroup.com

The Vital Sap the Great Captains Tap

Tom Rumsey, the special ops officer now working at GE in team building, cited the following telling quote from Napoleon:

> Every soldier has a cup of courage, and can only pour till it's empty, and everyone has different-sized cups.

In the beginning of this book, we referred to how teams offer a special sauce, or a kind of organizational glue, that we all note but only a few can easily generate. It is not the charisma found in gifted individuals; it is a vital sap that oozes from the great teams between and within the individuals like tales of the ancient Indian god Yakshi.

History portrays Yakshi as auspicious and fetching, a goddess who graces, for example, the east gateway of the Great Stupa at Sanchi from the years 50 BC to the present day India. She is shown as a graceful, seminude female figure, intimately and boldly entwined with a mango tree in legend.

But I want to you to visualize this goddess to make a more lasting impression on what I mean by the vital sap the great captains note and release in teams. This sensual force, Yakshi, according to Buddhist traditions from several regions, is an expression of the divine life force that surges through all things, especially as it is manifested in the growth and flowering of most forms of vegetative life.

Many Buddhists identify Yakshi with the life of a common tree in their backyard, for example, or their favorite tree in a park. In this view, they see the tree draws its sustenance directly from the subterranean waters absorbed through its roots, both invisible to the normal eye, and that this sauce or goo is transformed into a vital sap.

According to Buddhist theory (not contemporary science), the sap rises upon the will of Yakshi, channeled and propelled up the trunks of the tree toward the light. As it reaches to the fingers of the branches, like a fountain, it spills out invisibly, covering the branches of the tree and bringing the tree into maturity, which then allows the canopy of the tree, then the foliage, and soon enough the recurrent flowers and abundant fruit to bloom and proceed before all of us.

Captains create the special sauce in their teams. Some call it the chemistry of the team; others refer to it as momentum or the magic in their leadership. My point is this: whatever tradition you may prefer, the vital sap of Yakshi is more than a metaphor. It is something we see time and again in teams.

This very evident life force in teams drives the awakening of individuals. In Hinduism and in Buddhism, one never denies that this life force comes from individuals. But their discipline is to use it to direct and control the vital sap toward the goal of self-transcendence and liberation of the ego.

My book on teams is the farthest manifesto from a religious or spiritual tract. But many of us have heard Yakshi and her entrancing screams at night. She accosts us as world travelers and asks us to participate in this wheel of transcendence from the mere self.

I say this all with my tongue in my cheek. I find writing about this special sauce in teams fun. Many of my friends who are professional writers recommended that I delete these passages, claiming that they can later embarrass me. Yet I would prefer at this point to talk about this vital life force as a way for you to better appreciate the very common wonder in captains—captains understand where we stand.

The Universality in Teams and the Work of Captains

Everyone is capable of all three elements (the capacity for harm, generosity, and evil), and the captain influences how these elements are used. All competitors have these elements in their tool chests, too. The captain's role is to first recognize each person's ability and then determine what kind of guidance each person needs to liberate the needed percentages in the right situations.

The Circumstance and the Situation Is the Win

Again and again, the captain must recognize the times where harm or evil are actually needed and when they are not.

In my last three books, I deliberately suggest the management of harm and evil as near sisters. This phenomenon of a required great captain is again evident in sports teams.

We see it when a coach or team captain knows just what to say to the key shooter to motivate him enough to be aggressive in a shootout to decide a tie game. We see it as well when a coach is compelled to draw generosity from the point guard to pass to the right player instead of driving to the basket when it's necessary.

Top leaders possess this expert and conscious knowledge of when to utilize generosity, harm, or evil.

A Political Example in Grant and Lincoln

Abraham Lincoln took this role of captain over the Union, balancing and guiding his subordinates through the Civil War. Lincoln wrote a letter to General Ulysses S. Grant after the battle of Vicksburg, the bloodiest of all battles in the Civil War, admitting that he had questioned whether Grant's overly aggressive and violent strategy was indeed harmful. At the same time, Lincoln found the generosity of language to compliment Grant, saying that he had the right mix of capabilities to win the war.

Although Grant's barbaric bloodshed was excessive, it was unfortunately needed at the time to win the war.

In this letter, Lincoln informed Grant that he was making him the top of all generals. Lincoln understood that Grant was capable of generosity but also capable of harm and putting men at "necessary risk." Although Lincoln was known as one of the most generous and honest of men, he recognized that the capacity for harm and evil were required under the circumstances. This is not the way most people imagine Lincoln, even today, but it is the very essence of what made him great.

Although it might sound surprising or even extreme, successful executives need this capacity for generosity, harm, and evil as well. Professionals and leaders in various fields often have exceptional talent and the generous ability to lead others but lack the capacity to generate harm—and therefore fail to perform needed actions.

Lincoln recognized the consequences of appointing Grant as head of the generals. He felt that with Grant as their leader, all the generals would have the ability, through the combined characteristics of a team, to become skilled officers at Grant's level. Lincoln was also aware that other generals were jealous of Grant. He knew that they said he was evil and took too many risks, but he made a conscious choice to appoint Grant as head general, knowing that a brutal leader was required to take action against the enemy they had in General Robert E. Lee.

Working Your Generals, a True Captain at Work

Lincoln wrote another letter to two competing key generals, William T. Sherman and Grant, during this time of crisis. This letter was about organizational coherence and integrity of the full team. He handed to them—as a *team*—the decision of what to do next. Doing so was a brilliant action as a leader and shows that Lincoln was capable of generosity as well as harm.

Others were not capable of the violence and harm required. Lincoln was looking for the right kind of person to do this, someone who could take the violent action necessary against General Robert E. Lee without instruction. Lincoln recognized Grant's hubris; however, he used it to his advantage by allowing Grant to dictate his own means, while at the same time guiding Grant's self-assurance toward the unified corporate mission.

Lincoln forced the two men, who had previously been working *against* each other for individual motives, to mend their differences and unite to win the war.

Thanks to Lincoln's letters, Grant and Sherman were compelled to combine their abilities, set goals, and become results-oriented toward a unified end. Lincoln's mind was on the grave conditions that the war presented and the administrative obstacles he had to face to succeed. Above all, Lincoln was on a "corporate mission" to keep the nation together, much like a CEO or industry leader, and he communicated the importance of that mission to all his subordinates.

Unified goals—that special sauce in all the great teams—were the glue that held together the forces within Lincoln's cabinet and among his generals, motivating them and keeping them focused on the mission. Using subtle praise of the actions and characteristics he favored and thoughtful warning or encouragement to improve on weaknesses, Lincoln successfully guided his generals and the nation through turmoil.

Lincoln used his knowledge of human nature, along with his skills in guidance and persuasion, to create a shared goal for all his generals and cabinet members: keeping the Union intact and winning the war. He knew that his leadership held a unified focus and motivation toward the needed direction. Lincoln needed his subordinates to get a job done, and he had both the psychological acuity and the rhetorical skill to call on them to use both their strengths and their weaknesses to achieve the goal.

The Real Penalty Facing Joe Paterno's Penn State Football Teams

Once again, my day of musing about great teams has been interrupted by reality. Lately, I have been balancing my consulting travel and book speaking engagements so that I have nearly two billable days per week to write. And then reality speaks more loudly . . .

I am writing this chapter on July 24, 2012, and today, you cannot turn on the media without finding news coverage on Penn State and its football team. The *New York Times* just featured a news analysis by Pete Thamel about the "real penalty for Penn State" among the historic penalties facing the school's football program. This scenario clearly represents humans' capacity for harm, Joe Paterno's refusal to recognize it, and then his administration's and team's failure to recognize the capacity for evil.

The language of the National Collegiate Athletic Association (NCAA) bosses who handed down the sanctions was, as Thamel reported, "unrelievedly grim."

They labeled the sexual abuse scandal as "the worst chapter in the history of intercollegiate athletics." They wondered if there were other programs that had gotten too big to fail and offered stern warnings not only through the $60 million fine—a year's worth of earnings—but also by stripping the legendary Joe Paterno of his title as the top-winning coach.

To quote Thamel:

The sanctions follow an independent report commission-ed by the university's board of trustees and compiled by

Louis J. Freeh, a former F. B. I. director, that **found a culture of football reverence and a fear of bad publicity led administrators at the highest level to fail to report** the former coach Jerry Sandusky's attacks on children to authorities.

Clearly, those of you who may have disagreed with my earlier claims that there is a Macho Paradox in teams may want to revisit your position. The captains who succeed more than average, who win more than they lose, must liberate the capacity of generosity in their teams by controlling—and at times, completely repressing—the capacity for evil.

Keeping this ability to repress evil in mind, we can play the game of the modern corporation with less scandal. We can compete for limited resources with some sound recourse to law and standard setting, and we can certify and verify a fair playing field.

If we expect anything less of the coach, of our captains, that is what we will get—something so much less than what society expects that it will withstand nothing and collapse over time.

Tips on Bad Teams

It is very important that in a world of 7 billion souls that we learn from past examples of bad teamwork. I have written about Penn State, Lance Armstrong, and a few bad apples for a reason.

No one—from Joe Paterno to Lance Armstrong—is completely above the team. You see that there is only harm and bad consequences when superstar coaches such as Joe Paterno or superstar achievers such as Lance Armstrong find themselves defending what is no longer tenable to defend.

We all can be snookered in our common desire to admire victors—that's what life brings to the competitor, and only the true team competitor finds the strength to resist the corruption and the wrong.

Applying Teams to Profit Making

Improving profit margins really boils down to three things:

1. Improving the overall smoothness of the key teams, from the leadership councils to the business unit and deployment teams

2. Through the tools of benchmarking and leadership engagement, visualizing the superior team approach—what many call corporate vision and corporate strategy

3. Giving the key captains of the firm authority to align and to make accountable those capable of evil, harm, and generosity

You see all of this in the tale "Swift-Runner and the Trickster Tarantula." We learn more from this kind of positive reflection than from the far more entertaining horrors of Lance Armstrong's team or the dark and deviant evidence of deliberate blindnesses in the Penn State macho culture.

Credo and Finale

For in the end, teams are like a fine stereo system.

You stand before them and say, "Well, that sounds right!" High fidelity is achieved by the careful alignment and synchronization of the key component parts of the living team.

As you finish this book, ask yourself these three things:

1. **Who forms the core components of this high fidelity at my firm?** Cultivate those key folks like lifelong friends or

marriage partners. For in the end, how they sound is how you sound as you grow in revenue, reputation, and society at large.

2. **How do I reinforce the desires and goals of my key team players, and how do I sync that with the entire organization?** Think of this as something you ask yourself each quarter, as if in a 48-minute basketball game.

3. **Does my team system sound right?** In the end, we want a team system that sounds right. It must sound very right indeed to your investors, your customers, and your stakeholders. Since teams are watched constantly internally and externally, this is more important than all the other measures and all the evidence of short-term returns. It must sound and look right, as a team. It must be smooth, be coherent, and have integrity each time it is engaged.

Finally, the many great corporate mansions I have visited in my work achieve results in this high fidelity way through teams.

As we warned in Part I of this book, to think otherwise is to overvalue the intellectual property, technology, and distribution routes for your wealth. I sometimes wonder if this will be documented in the devaluation of Facebook's stock upon its famous initial public offering (IPO) launch.

It is in your team that your value resides—as you have worked so hard to ascertain and to control its parts and its players. So work each engaged hour to keep it humming.

A Return to Our Beginning

As I mentioned in my prior book *Doing More with Less*, today's swifter and more severe globalized world requires that we compete like Benjamin Franklin all over again. We must rely on teams to be frugal, diplomatic, and inventive—not just remain pre-occupied with our own short life's solo trajectory.

We need to realign our money, people, teams, and rules with competitive urgency in mind. The hours of a day are short, and our lives slip by. But the larger purpose of teams mounts in momentum and consequence if captained with grace, force, and fascination.

In teamwork, wrongs must be righted, and justice in the end must prevail. By learning how to humble himself from the early mistakes, by maturing in his asking up the chain of friends to help him out of the mess, our humble Swift-Runner has his problems solved by a well-functioning high-performing team full of diverse help and multiple meanings. It has always been this way. It can be no other way. Await your chance to captain teams. It will come by several times for you.

True accomplishment in teams is more about the pleasures of maturation. The magic in teams does not reside in the simple counting of the statistics of individuals, nor in the mindless counting of short-lived victories.

In great teamwork, we extend our wings.

APPENDIX

Bruce Piasecki's Core Team

The AHC Group

www.ahcgroup.com

Bruce Piasecki
Founder & President
www.brucepiasecki.com
www.DoingMoreWith
LessBook.com

Dr. Bruce Piasecki is the President and founder of AHC Group, Inc., a management consulting firm specializing in energy, materials, and environmental corporate matters—whose clients include Suncor Energy, Hess, FMC, the Warren Buffett firm Shaw Industries, Toyota, and other global companies in his Corporate Affiliates training workshops.

Dr. Piasecki is the author of several seminal books on business strategy, valuation, and corporate change, including the Nature Society's book of the year, *In Search of Environmental Excellence: Moving*

Beyond Blame as well as the recent *New York Times, USA Today,* and *Wall Street Journal* bestseller *Doing More with Less.*

Since 1981, he has advised companies about the critical areas of corporate governance, energy, environmental strategy, product innovation, and sustainability strategy with his teams of Senior Associates. See www.ahcgroup.com for more details.

Steven W. Percy
AHC Group Senior Associate
www.worldincbook.com

Key AHC Group Assignments

- Mentoring leaders to become CEOs
- Increasing AHC Group Workshop members' diversity and range

Steve Percy is the former Chairman and CEO of BP America, Inc., BP's US subsidiary prior to its merger with Amoco Corporation, and served in that capacity from 1996 until 1999. Prior to assuming those duties, he was President of BP Oil in the United States from 1992 to 1996. Mr. Percy returned to BP America in 1992 from London, England, where he served as Group Treasurer of The British Petroleum Company p.l.c. and Chief Executive of BP Finance International.

Since retiring from BP he has served as the head of Phillips Petroleum's Refining, Marketing and Transportation Company, visited as a Professor of Corporate Strategy and International Business at the University of Michigan Graduate School of Business, and conducted workshops on corporate governance for the AHC Group.

Mr. Percy is currently contributing to the Millennium Ecosystem Assessment of the United Nations as Coordinating Lead Author with respect to its Conceptual Framework and its

Responses working group as well as leading the writing of its synthesis report for business and industry.

Mr. Percy is currently is a member of the Board of Directors of Omnova Solutions Inc. and is Non-executive Chairman of Wavefront Energy and Environmental Services Inc., a Canadian company that has developed and commercialized innovative technologies for fluid flow and process monitoring in the environmental and energy sectors.

Kenneth Strassner
AHC Group Senior Associate
ken@ahcgroup.com

Key AHC Group Assignments

- Workshop Chair for "Competing on Sustainability" and Facilitator for Stakeholder Engagement Workshop

- Hess, Suncor, and select sustainability and growth councils

An AHC Group Senior Associate since 2009, Kenneth Strassner is an honors graduate (magna cum laude) of Yale College (1968) and of Yale Law School (1974).

Prior to joining Kimberly-Clark Corporation in 1976, Mr. Strassner served as an officer in the US Navy. He also practiced with a law firm in Washington, DC and served as Executive Assistant to the Assistant Secretary of Labor for Occupational Safety and Health. His legal specialties include US and international environmental and energy law, product safety matters, and occupational safety and health requirements.

In 1988, Mr. Strassner was appointed Vice President— Environment and Energy at Kimberly-Clark Corporation, with responsibility for formulation of corporate policies and management of the company's technical support staffs in both areas. From 2004 to 2008, he served as Vice President—Global Environment, Safety, Regulatory and Scientific Affairs for Kimberly-Clark. In this role he managed the development of Kimberly-Clark's Corporate and Business Unit sustainability plans as well as relationships with outside stakeholders interested in the corporation's sustainability performance.

Gerald I. Bresnick
AHC Group Senior Associate
gerald@ahcgroup.com

Key AHC Group Assignments

- Executive Director AHC Group Training Institute; and Workshop Chair on "Emerging Issues"
- DTE, on reputation and selective engagement

Gerald I. (Gerry) Bresnick was most recently the Corporate Vice President for Environment, Health, Safety and Social Responsibility at Hess Corporation prior to joining the AHC Group as a Senior Associate.

Prior to joining Hess, Mr. Bresnick was the US Director of Health, Safety and Environment for BP, headquartered in Chicago. He joined BP following its merger with Amoco Corporation in 1998.

During his 18 years with Amoco, he was involved in all areas of environment, health, and safety. His assignments ranged from Manager of EH&S for the Amoco Chemicals Company to Director of Corporate Medical Services as well as leading Amoco's Product Stewardship program.

Mr. Bresnick has worked on projects for and with various governments, NGOs, and international agencies around the world. He has served as Chair or Co-Chair of trade association committees dealing with all areas of health, safety, environment, and social impact from oil and petrochemical operations and has spoken at various national and international meetings and conferences. He is the author of numerous studies and reports and several papers in the peer-reviewed literature and is a frequent speaker at professional society meetings and college seminars.

A. Dwight Bedsole
AHC Group Senior Associate
www.worldincbook.com

Key AHC Group Assignments

- Workshop Chair on "Site Remediation and Risk Reduction"
- Client services include work at the board level in governance (Agrium and others) and with a multinational chemical company to develop and implement a sustainable growth program for their global operations by chartering task groups for internal and external stakeholder engagement, defining global mega-trends to identify potential risks and opportunities, designing a process for business integration, setting goals and metrics to measure progress, and developing a framework for sustainability reporting.
- Client development

Dwight Bedsole retired with over 39 years of experience with DuPont in a variety of production, R&D, technical, project design/liaison, business, and environmental management roles.

While at DuPont, Mr. Bedsole participated in the formation and management of DuPont Environmental Remediation Services (DERS) and chartered and managed the DuPont Corporate Remediation Group. Dwight led this group for 17 years in the management of DuPont's global environmental remediation liabilities with an annual expenditure of approximately $100 million, and liability estimated between $350 million and $1.2 billion.

As a Business Director for a global business, Mr. Bedsole also led the Strategic Planning Process for Marketing, R&D, and Manufacturing and the complete restructuring of global business.

Mr. Bedsole worked with the US EPA, State Department, and UN to negotiate the chlorofluorocarbon (CFC) global phase-out plan with the international community (Montreal Protocol)—Corporate Environmental Respect Award. Additionally, at the invitation of the UK government, he participated in the investigation of the Flixborough disaster (1974 vapor cloud explosion at a caprolactam plant).

Steve Willis
AHC Group Senior Associate
www.ahcgroup.com
www.CorporateConsulting
Group.com

Key AHC Group Assignments

- Workshop Chair on "Delivering on the Bottom Line"
- Facilitator in benchmarking project relative to Long Term Stewardship for seven firms, including Freeport McMoRan Copper & Gold
- Client development

Before joining the AHC Group in 2007, Steve was the Global Director of Whirlpool Corporation's health, safety, and environmental (HSE) management system, having retired after 33 years of service, including over 22 years as the senior HSE professional for the corporation.

Prior to Whirlpool, Mr. Willis had seven years of experience working for NASA on research projects involving regenerative life support systems for long-duration manned space flights at NASA's Langley Research Center in Virginia.

Mr. Willis's key career accomplishments include the conversion of an environmental management system from reactive to proactive mode focused on environmental risk management by minimizing the number of hazardous waste disposal facilities used and by eliminating use of PCB, TCE, asbestos, and underground storage tanks. He also led the evolution of Whirlpool's HSE management system as it grew from 10 US plants to plants in three countries in 1990 and to 65 plants in 14 countries in 2007.

Steve also developed and implemented detailed global HSE standards and provided consistent, high-level environmental protection in all countries, even where existing laws were not sufficiently protective.

Greg Dixon
AHC Group Senior Associate
www.ahcgroup.com

Key AHC Group Assignments

- Project Leader on various workshops including Stakeholder Engagement, annual event involving dozens of global companies from Disney to HP, PSEG, and others at www.ahcgroup.com

- Research analysis pursuant to specific client needs

Greg Dixon is the Managing Partner of Noonmark Group, LLC, a strategic marketing, consulting, and research firm specializing in tourism and economic development.

Prior to joining AHC Group in 2011, Mr. Dixon served as Vice President of Tourism at the Saratoga County Chamber of Commerce in Saratoga Springs, New York. In his role there, he led the tourism marketing program for Saratoga County and Saratoga Springs, which included the direction of all media buying, branding, public relations, advertising and marketing planning, internet marketing strategy, and destination research programs.

Mr. Dixon works with the AHC Group on the development and coordination of its Stakeholder Engagement Executive Briefings, research projects, and for AHC Group clients on reputation, branding, and communications strategies relating to sustainable business practices and community engagement.

Kate Schrank
AHC Group Senior Associate

Key AHC Group Assignments

- Supports AHC in financial, strategic and legal issues for our clients and affiliates
- Support of Corporate Affiliate membership growth with special financial and sustainability disclosure expertise regarding Bloomberg terminal and others investment trends

Katherine (Kate) Schrank, JD is founder and President of Sustainability Partners, Inc., a boutique consulting firm that works with organizations (profit and nonprofit) that want to increase profitability while using their influence to make the world a better place. Her reputation is one for getting things done by thinking strategically and practically to her client's advantage.

Kate Schrank practiced environmental law for over 15 years, successfully resolving complex environmental issues for a range of industries, with a focus on regulatory compliance and beyond. She has extensive experience working with multiple stakeholders (business people, scientists, engineers, counsel, government, and NGOs) to achieve results for her clients. This background provides her with a deep foundation and context for advising organizations that want to develop and implement sustainability strategies and best practices. She is certified as a sustainability practitioner by the Institute of Environmental Management and Assessment (IEMA) based in London, which provides a focus on global sustainability trends, measurement, and reporting. For her LinkedIn profile, visit www.linkedin.com/in/sustainability partnersinc.

Marti Simmons
Corporate Affiliates Director

Key AHC Group Assignments

- Development and management of the Corporate Affiliates Program (www.ahcgroup.com)
- Research and administrative support to the entire AHC team
- Coordinator of dozens of contractors relative to legal, accounting, web design, and video

Near Future Training

Near Future Training

There are a set of core competencies that the next generation of business managers need to be in command of.

The AHC Group is positioned to help promising leaders from your firm achieve the essential skills needed to manage at the highest level. If you believe that existing internal mentoring and training programs meet most of your succession and review needs, but more focused development could be helpful, please contact us today.

The AHC Group Senior Associates each have years of experience at major companies as leaders of their EHS and Sustainability programs. The real world experience of these Senior Associates includes development and delivery of corporate wide and global training programs on policies and specific technical subjects, managing and facilitating internal benchmarking sessions, focused process improvement workshops, and individual mentoring for high potential employees.

OBJECTIVES OF THE AHC TRAINING INSTITUTE

For the sponsoring companies: Strengthen the capabilities of the strongest Energy, Product and Environment Sustainability practitioners, and others who are or may become involved in this area, to achieve breakthrough performance for their companies. Help insure successful compliance with the aggressive performance targets set by the company. Emphasize the need to measure and articulate the business value of sustainability initiatives to senior leaders and others within the company, as well as to external audiences.

For the participants: Continue development of knowledge and leadership skills necessary for employees to make greater contributions to their company, and to perform at their maximum potential.

> Our Cornerstone Integrative Classes are based on the principles of
> *Doing More with Less* and *Doing More with Teams*

Near Future Training

SCOPE OF TRAINING

This training curriculum will offer one or two day sessions at least twice a year over three years. Some companies may cherry pick from the individual sessions, depending on their needs. Maximum benefit for the sponsoring companies and the individual participants will come from involvement in the full three year program.

Between sessions, the participants will apply the knowledge they have learned in the sessions to undertake meaningful projects on the job, and well as assignments within the group participating in the training program. The AHC Coaches will work with the participants between sessions on a one-on-one basis and with the participants as a group, to discuss individual and team assignments, and situations encountered on the job that relate to the training sessions. The AHC Coaches will also hold discussions periodically with the participant and their company mentor to assess progress and establish measurable goals that demonstrate that the program and the participant are making appropriate progress.

SUGGESTIONS FOR THE SPONSORING COMPANY

To achieve maximum effectiveness, the sponsoring company should assign an internal mentor, not necessarily that participant's supervisor, to counsel and guide the employee in matters relating to the training program, and to team with the AHC Coach to assure that satisfactory progress related to the training program is being achieved.

Since 1981 the AHC Group, a general management consulting firm headquartered outside Saratoga Springs, New York, has specialized in the critical areas of corporate governance consulting , energy and environmental strategy, product innovation, and sustainability strategy. Through our consulting contracts, business leadership seminars, and strategy and growth publications, we have helped hundreds of companies to realize the business potential in environmental and public issues, enhance stakeholder and investor relations, and position themselves better in the marketplace.

www.ahcgroup.com

Near Future Training

AHC GENERAL TRAINING CURRICULUM

Overview of Energy, Environmental, and Product Sustainability Leadership

- Introduction to the three year program
- Unique skills and abilities needed by EHS & Sustainability practitioners
- Unique stakeholder expectations for a company's EHS & S performance
- Characteristics of successful leaders
- Enablers and barriers to success
- Techniques for developing leadership skills

Exercising Judgment

- Seeing the Bigger picture
- Managing Complexity, Coping with Uncertainty
- Earning buy-in by senior managers and other influencers in the company
- Leading Change
- Strategy versus Tactics
- Short term versus Long Term
- Understanding your role in the process
- Arguing versus Collaborating
- Resolving conflict
- Finding common ground

Making the Case in your Company for That Innovative Idea

- Being an effective advocate
- Understanding the audience, their goals, perspectives, culture, and language
- Crafting effective internal and external messages
- The Power of Benchmarking
- Avoiding annoyance
- Who are the champions and the blockers

Near Future Training

AHC GENERAL TRAINING CURRICULUM (continued)

Achieving Breakthrough Performance

- Why Leaders Matter
- The Myth of the Born Leader
- Envisioning a Future State
- From Management to Leadership
- The "Big Hairy Goal"
- Listen more – Talk Less
- Understanding team dynamics
- Sharing credit so that everyone is a winner
- Organizational Transformation and Culture Change

Measuring performance and success

- Setting S.M.A.R.T. goals
- Leading versus Lagging
- Qualitative versus Quantitative
- Hard versus Soft Benefits
- Performance Appraisals
- Coaching and Counseling

Partnerships

- The power of Strategic Partnerships
- Finding the Right Partners, internally and externally
- Why alliances fail
- Understanding the "Prisoners Dilemma"
- Getting to "Win–Win"

Contact Bruce Piasecki at 518-583-9615
for an orientation to these sessions.

Also by Bruce Piasecki

Doing More with Less: The New Way to Wealth (Hoboken, NJ: John Wiley & Sons, 2012).

The Surprising Solution: Creating Possibility in a Swift and Sever World (New York: Sourcebooks, 2010).

World, Inc. (New York: Sourcebooks, 2007).

Environmental Management and Business Strategy: Leadership Skills for the 21st Century (New York: John Wiley & Sons, 1998).

Corporate Environmental Strategy: The Avalanche of Change Since Bhopal (New York: John Wiley & Sons, 1995).

In Search of Environmental Excellence: Moving Beyond Blame (New York: Simon & Schuster, 1990).

America's Future in Toxic Waste Management: Lessons from Europe (Westport, CT: Quorum Books, 1987).

Beyond Dumping: New Strategies for Controlling Toxic Contamination (Westport, CT: Quorum Books, 1984).

Corporate Strategy Today (CST). A monograph series published by the AHC Group, Inc. Titles include:

Leading Corporate Strategies and Climate Change: A Few Key Business Examples (AHC Group, 2006).

The Path to Growth: Building Corporate Value Through Social Leadership (AHC Group, 2005).

Corporate Environmental Strategy: The Journal of Environmental Leadership. Founding Editor, issues 1–46.

Index